PASSI<
PLAN,
PROFIT

PASSION, PLAN, PROFIT

Twelve Simple Steps
to Convert Your Passion
into a Solid Business

Christy Strauch

Creative
Peace
Press

PASSION, PLAN, PROFIT: Twelve Simple Steps to Convert Your Passion into a Solid Business
© 2009–2020 Christy Strauch

Published by:
Creative Peace Press
5601 N. 79th St #4
Scottsdale, AZ 85250

ISBN: 978-1-7347365-0-2

Cover design: The Book Designers

Text design and composition: OneVoiceCan.com

Printed in the U.S.A.

First Printing, September 2020

Contents

When love and skill work together,
expect a masterpiece.

—JOHN RUSKIN

Acknowledgments

Thanks first to Jim Horan, whose brilliant book, *The One Page Business Plan*, showed me and thousands of others that it was possible to write a powerful business plan that was also simple and easy to use. Next, Leslie Keenan, whose steadfast vision, support and encouragement motivated me to finish this book, as well as Michelle Radomski, who inspired me to revise it. Thanks to Julia McNeal for ruthless editing (twice!); The Book Designers for a professional, yet eccentric cover design, Cecile Duhnke, Barbara Bitondo, and Laura DeVault for critical read-throughs, and Joe Radomski for the beautiful, clean interior. Thanks to Matt MacEachern for coming up with the killer title, and Dad for reading proof after proof after proof. Those accounting classes of yours came in handy.

I especially thank everyone who test-drove this book while I was writing it, and then actually purchased and used the book during the ten years since the first edition was published. Your suggestions, criticism, enthusiasm and ongoing support are why I wrote the book in the first place, and why I am updating it now. More than ever, we need you to be prosperous and sustainable doing the work you love. Your work matters.

Preface

There is a vitality, a life force, an energy, a quickening, that is translated through
you into action, and because there is only one of you in all time, this expression is unique.
And if you block it, it will never exist through any other medium and will be lost.

MARTHA GRAHAM

Many people fear, or even completely avoid, trying to make a living doing the things they do best—the work that calls to them from their heart. This is because the scariest thing in the world is to go after what the deepest part of you wants, and risk failing at it. I created this workbook because I strongly believe that given the right tools, along with accountability and persistence, you can succeed, and more importantly, prosper, doing the work you were put on the planet to do.

You may have already tried to support yourself, and your family, doing the work you love, and failed. You believed that if you "do what you love, the money will follow." But it didn't work out for you. Your heart might be broken and you don't want to try again.

Here's the thing I want you to know. You didn't fail because you're stupid, or bad or ignorant or any of the other things your head might have told you. You failed because you didn't understand how to market consistently to your best prospects, how to price your goods and services correctly, how to watch your sales and expenses and get clear about what makes you different from your competitors.

This workbook is intended to help you.

You love what you do, and you're really good at it. That's a great start, but it's not enough. What will be different from here forward is that you now have the tools to bring two vital factors—clarity and accountability—to your life's work.

Loving what you do and excelling at it forms the necessary foundation for your business to succeed. This workbook will lead you through the steps to build the rest of the house.

Completing this workbook will force you to become very clear about how much your business must sell of its products and services; who your perfect customers are; and what makes you different from everyone else in the same business. This work can be challenging, and intimidating too. But it's worse not to try at all, to miss offering your best gifts to the world.

Join me in committing fully to the work you were meant to do. The tools to help you succeed, and a framework to keep you accountable, are contained in these pages. You provide the persistence, the commitment, and the love.

Download the worksheets, business plan template and updated resource list at www.christystrauch.com/books. Your work matters. Let's get started.

Christy Strauch
2020

Introduction

The underlying premise of this book is that *Clarity is Good*. More specifically, clarity about your numbers is *very good*.

When you go through this workbook and do the work, you will get deep clarity about your business.

What is clarity, anyway? Clarity is knowing:

The purpose of your business.

How much money you need to generate each month to pay your bills and put aside some for a rainy day.

Who your best customers are.

How your customers like you to talk to them.

What prices you need to charge to stay in business.

And loads of other essential information that you will know when you finish this work.

Here are some specific examples of how Clarity is Good:
Clarity about your numbers can tell you if a marketing idea works or not.

The writing genius who helped me finish this book, started marketing her business of helping people write their books, using a traditional method that everyone said she should use: print and direct-mail a fancy (expensive) brochure. She also began teaching writing classes.

Because she tracked where her clients came from (most from her writing classes and not many at all from the brochures) and she knew how much it cost to put on the classes *and* how much it cost to print and mail the brochures, she realized, classes: *good*; mailing brochures (especially to the wrong people): *bad*.

Having the brochures turned out to be useful in an unexpected way. Because they listed her class schedule, people who were already in her classes wanted the brochures to keep track of her teaching schedule, and to give them to other people they knew who were interested in writing a book of their own. It turned out that mailing the brochures to people didn't work, but handing them out to existing clients (her students) did. She would not have known this information had she not tracked how her clients came to her.

Knowing how much it cost to generate leads, both from the brochures and from the classes, plus keeping track of where her clients came from, told her how to market. Clarity guided her efforts into the marketing channels that were the most productive.

Clarity about your numbers can tell you how much money you can earn under your current pricing plan, with the number of people who work for you.

One of my clients who owns a cleaning service, wanted to create enough sales in her business so that she could take home $100,000 in salary. After factoring in all her business expenses and using the hourly rate she currently charged her clients, the numbers told her she would have to work 5,000 hours a year to net the $100,000.

Since there are only 2,000 work hours in a year, she realized she had to do something differently: raise her prices, hire more help, or offer more services to her current clients that someone besides her would deliver. Clarity about her numbers told her exactly what she needed to do (and what wouldn't work) to hit her earning goal.

Clarity about your numbers can tell you whether to pursue a new product line or not.

Another client was solicited by a company who wanted her to sell their products to her clients. On the surface it looked like a good idea. Her clients already purchased products similar to this company's goods, and being associated with this new company would lend credibility to her business.

But when she sat down and calculated how much she would earn selling these products, she realized that for the amount of time it took to sell the products and at the commission rate the company paid her, she would barely make minimum wage. Clarity kept her from wasting her time.

Clarity about how much money you need to pay your bills and save for the future, as well as knowing where your sales will come from, frees up vast frontiers of creative space in your brain. When you know what your money situation is, you can let go and do the work you love.

You may not have experienced this feeling of clarity very frequently, but I'm guessing you've experienced its evil twin: obsession about making enough money, and vagueness about how much you have in your checking account, savings account, etc. That mindset is the death of creativity.

I am inviting you to use this book to clear away that chaos so you can be free to create.

Once you finish the business plan in this book, to maintain your clarity, I will also ask you to review your plan, monthly and quarterly. There are forms at the back of the book that will help you with this process.

I have learned from teaching many business-plan workshops that there is huge value in doing a business plan. That value increases exponentially when you review the plan, and make the changes that you need to make, based on what your customers really want, and what the marketplace is telling you.

Let this book take you through creating a plan you can use to operate your business. If you get stuck anywhere in the process that follows, remember why you're doing this work: to create clarity in your business so you can be free to do the work you were put here to do, and to prosper doing that work.

Read This Before You Begin

There's one thing you need before you begin this business plan workbook. In order for the plan to work, for it to help you build a successful business, your business must be turning out high-quality products and services, and delivering them professionally.

If your clients aren't telling you how wonderful you are at least once a week, or they're complaining about an aspect of your products or services, you must fix this. You can (and should) still create your business plan, but your number-one goal (in Module Twelve: Goals and Plans) must be to repair any problems. Your clients must love you.

Note: You may have some clients you can't please no matter what you do. You have my permission to let those clients go. You're not trying to wow everyone, just your perfect clients.

If you have any questions about whether your clients do love you, ask them. There are two, free Internet-based customer survey tools in the Resources section in the back of the book. But if you really want to know, take your five best clients to breakfast or lunch (one at a time) and ask them face-to-face. Unless they're on the verge of firing you, they'll be glad of the attention and even happier that they can help you improve.

If you think you might get negative feedback, you might need to get some psychic encouragement before you talk to your clients. Do whatever you need to do so you can sit through honest feedback from them without flinching or becoming defensive (or crying, as I once did).

If you are just starting your business, you have homework also. You must start trying out your business idea on real customers as soon as possible. Tell your guinea pigs that you're experimenting on them and in exchange for a low price for your product/service, you will want to gather detailed feedback from them. Try out as many of your ideas as possible and see what your potential clients say about them.

You can have an amazing idea for a business, but you must insure that people are interested in your products and services. The sooner you find out what your clients like and don't like, the faster your business will be profitable and successful. And if you've already got a stable of great products and services but you aren't delivering them well, fix that. The best business plan in the world won't remedy either of these problems. Only you can.

Caution

"Late at night have you experienced a vision of the person you might become, the work you could accomplish, the realized being you were meant to be? Are you a writer who doesn't write, a painter who doesn't paint, an entrepreneur who never starts a venture? Then you know what Resistance is.

Resistance is the most toxic force on the planet. It is the root of more unhappiness than poverty, disease and erectile dysfunction. To yield to Resistance deforms our spirit. It stunts us and makes us less than we are and were born to be. If you believe in God (and I do) you must declare Resistance evil, for it prevents us from achieving the life God intended when He endowed each of us with our own unique genius."

STEVEN PRESSFIELD, *THE WAR OF ART*

When you embark on a new mission (or begin really paying attention to the mission you're already involved in), something interesting almost always happens:

Fear tries to stop you in your tracks.

There are various names for this phenomenon. In the coaching business, this voice that tells you, loudly or softly, persuasively, insidiously, that if you try this new thing, you're going to fail and *fail big*, is called the "gremlin" or "saboteur."

Steven Pressfield, the author of *The Legend of Bagger Vance* and other great books, calls it Resistance. Some people (including Pressfield) even call this phenomenon evil. It may manifest in your life as a voice in your head whispering that you'd better not take this risk to make a living doing what you love, because you might fail. You may also hear this voice whispering something along the lines of:

"How could I ask someone to pay me for this work? It's so much fun I'd do it for free."

Or: "This work is so easy; anybody could do it. Why would someone pay for this?"

Your saboteur might take the form of roadblocks that seem to arise just as you get close to your goal. It may even show up dressed as your mother, father, ex-sweetheart, ex-husband, wife, partner (or worse, current wife, husband or partner) who says things like: "Are you sure you're ready? Is this what you really want? Are you equipped to handle all this?" Or other questions along these lines that may sound halfway reasonable but are simply meant to stop you from succeeding at this crucial venture.

What helps the most in dealing with the saboteur is to view it/her/him as simply the part of you that decided at age five that taking risks is way too scary, so you should never take any. Anytime this part of you smells a risk (and what could be riskier than making a living doing the work you love?), its voice will kick in to try and stop you. Its main goal is your safety, even at the expense of never living or working in your purpose, never creating a business doing the work you were put on the planet to do. Your saboteur is happiest when you are watching Reality TV. Eight to twelve hours a day.

When your saboteur tries to get in your way, thank him or her for her efforts to keep you safe, reassure her that all is well, and keep moving forward.

If you feel that what you're doing is so instinctive you can't understand why someone would pay you to do it for them; that is a strong indication that you're working in an area where you are very gifted and can be wildly successful. Let me repeat this: *If your work feels like playing, or flows easily or is intuitive to you, with focus and accountability you can become very successful at it.*

Your saboteur loves to confuse you by saying this work comes this naturally to everyone. That is a huge lie. If you doubt this, ask your friends. What you find so easy to do, they will cringe at doing. Work you find effortless, fun, that flows, that wins accolades, attracts your saboteur like flies to honey. The stronger the saboteur, the closer you're coming to your important work.

You might need to gather a cheerleading squad around you (make sure they'll tell you the truth as they cheer), but whatever you do, don't let this saboteur, gremlin, Resistance, stop you from fulfilling your mission. The world is *aching* for your skills. We desperately need you. Don't leave us wanting.

How To Use This Book

The best (but not the only) way to go through this workbook is together.

Some of the benefits of doing it in a group are obvious. You can support each other through the times when it feels like there aren't enough hours in the day to do this vital work. You can hold each other accountable. You can get candid feedback. It also might be more fun, which is always important!

There is another, more subtle reason for doing it in a group. Even though your group members will probably have different businesses from yours, some of the best marketing ideas (and other ideas, too) can come from businesses completely outside your niche. In my business plan workshops, the most fun thing is to watch the software engineer and the artist (or in one workshop, the computer geek and the belly dancer) working together. They each bring a completely new and valuable perspective to the other's work.

If you have the energy and motivation to create a group to work through this book together, try to round up at least six people (including yourself). Eight or ten is even better because you'll get more points of view, but six is a great place to start. Commit to each other to meet for two hours, once a week. You will finish (with a little work outside the hours of the meeting), in six weeks.

In choosing this group, the greater the variety of businesses (and business owners) you can invite, the better. You will be amazed at the ideas you glean from other entrepreneurs who know nothing about your business, and who can look at your situation free of the prejudices and preconceived ideas you may be operating with, that you don't even realize. Diversity in the owners themselves also lends to discovering new ideas.

If you can't get a group of people to do this with you, the second best way to do it is with another business owner as your partner. You can still keep each other accountable and have someone to bounce ideas off. As you would with meeting in a group, set aside two hours per week with your partner, and you will also finish in six weeks. It's also good for you to find a partner who is not in your business. In addition to the cross-pollination that will occur, you may feel more willing to disclose details about your business that you might not feel comfortable telling a possible competitor.

That said, if you can't get either of these scenarios to work, *do it alone*. It's much better to do it alone than not to do it at all. The workbook will lead you through the process of writing your business plan, whether you do it in a group or all by yourself. If you do it alone, set aside the two hours per week to work on your plan, and make these hours inviolable. In other words, no interruptions, and no excuses. If you work on your plan alone and your business is already up and running, ask your best clients to look at your output, especially your Values, Strategies, your Target Market and even your Goals and Plans for the year. I've found my clients sometimes know more about my business than I do, and are very willing to help. You can still create a powerful plan that will guide you through the next 12–24 months, even if the only person who ever sees the whole thing is you.

A note for everyone:

> Whether you're working in a group, with a partner, or alone, give yourself permission to tell the truth. If you work with other people, choose ones you're willing to disclose your warts to. This is not an exercise in image management. It's better to do it alone than to feel like you have to hide anything from your group or your partner.

Now that you've taken the "whole truth and nothing but the truth" vow, see where you fit into one of the four types of people I wrote this workbook to help. First, there is the person who is just starting a business. This book will work for you. You will also need to do supplemental research. The places in the workbook for you to branch out and do your research are marked throughout.

I am a firm believer in trying things first before investing a lot of money and time. I will be asking you to test your assumptions as you write your plan. This means you need to start thinking now about how you will discover whether there is demand for the products or services you want to sell. There will be some things you don't know yet; the workbook will help you discover what those things are and help you create a plan to learn what you need.

Second, you may already have a business up and running, and you realize you need a plan. This book will work for you. You will use your current data and experiences to see what works well and where you need to make changes.

Third, you may have started a business and failed at it. This book will work for you. Because you have (valuable) experience at doing things that don't work, you will draw on that experience to create a business that does work.

Finally, you may have a successful business and want to start another one, or an offshoot of the one you have now. You are a cross between someone who is starting a new business and someone already in business. You will be able to use some of your existing experiences, and you will need to do research also. The workbook will help you see where you can use what you already know, and where you need to get more information.

My guarantee: If you do all the work in this book and fill in the business-plan template provided at the back of the book, you will create a plan that you can use to manage your business.

There are many forces, trends, market, and economic conditions that are out of our control as business owners. This workbook, and the completed business plan that you will create using this book, will guarantee that you are committed to being responsible for the part that you *can* control.

A Note About Resources

All the worksheets and spreadsheet templates along with an updated list of resources, are downloadable at www.christystrauch.com/books.

Everything Is Connected

Let's get started.

I wrote a story on the following pages that illustrates the foundation of this workbook: Namely, that all the aspects of the business plan you are about to write flow from one place—the purpose.

I used to feel guilty about this discovery and tried to disguise it from people in my workshops. It seemed too woo-woo, too touchy-feely. But I couldn't deny the truth of it. All aspects of a useful, resonant business plan flow from the purpose. Essentially: "Why you? Why this business? Why now?"

I could talk about the reason your business purpose is important from a spiritual standpoint, but I will leave that for you to discover for yourself if you wish.

The business reason that your purpose is important is because it guides your decision-making in every area of your business.

When you make decisions based on your purpose, your business becomes congruent. All the parts make sense, everything works together. What you say you do, and what you actually do, match. This is powerfully attractive to clients, employees, vendors, and everyone else.

Read the story that follows to see what I mean. As you read, begin to think about the underlying purpose for your business, and how you will articulate it to the outside world.

Everything Is Connected—A Story

Imagine you are a plumber. You work for someone. He's a great guy, but he skimps on the parts he uses. He buys whatever's cheapest.

It's not like he's dishonest. He tells the builders he works for exactly what kind of parts he's using. Their primary focus is profitability. They don't care.

But you don't like it. This is not how you like to work. You're a craftsman. Your work, and the parts you use in your work, create a job that's meant to last decades, maybe even a hundred years.

You wake up one morning and realize you can't work for this guy anymore. Your desire to build something that lasts is too strong.

You decide to go into business for yourself.

You are a person who does work that lasts, who uses the highest quality parts, who goes the extra mile. You need to be involved in a business that supports who you are. This is your *purpose* for starting your own business. This goes in the circle in the upper left corner of the diagram on page xxviii.

From your purpose, many other things will flow. The first is your Unique Selling Proposition: what's unique about you, compared to all other people in your same line of work? Based on your purpose, here's the answer: You are a craftsman. You are the person a builder calls when he wants the job done right. When a construction company needs someone who will attend to all the details, who will do a job that lasts, they will call you.

Your purpose also tells you who your perfect clients will be. In your case, you want to work with high-end builders and homeowners who care about quality. Chances are good these people will be building expensive homes. Perhaps you focus on commercial builders who must build structures to last for 100 years. You don't focus on low-profit, high volume business. Those clients don't fit your purpose.

Based on your purpose, what are your business strategies? Perhaps you help your clients understand why more expensive, high-quality parts are better. You educate. Your website is filled with information your customers can use to understand why you work the way you do, and why it's better for them. You give speeches at builders' conventions, educating them on the latest trends in plumbing. You join the local builders' association. They know you as someone who can answer any question about quality plumbing.

What are your values? Because you value quality and good workmanship so highly, perhaps your first value is integrity. Your clients and vendors know they can rely on you to tell them the truth. The value of integrity may lead you to take only jobs that fit your quality criteria. You don't take jobs that don't fit your model.

Knowing your purpose and your values, how much money do you want to make? How big do you want to be? Do many existing plumbing contractors cut corners? Is there room for a nationwide company that doesn't work that way. Is that you? Perhaps you know four builders in your city who do work that you admire, and you want to be the preferred plumbing contractor for those four companies alone. Is that your vision?

Knowing all these things—your vision, your values, your strategies, what's unique about you, and of course your underlying purpose—will lead directly into your income and spending plan (sometimes called a forecast, a budget, or an income forecast). Since you want to use high quality parts and do a high-quality job, those costs must be factored into your prices and your profit margins.

Knowing all these things also informs your marketing plan. You know you want to work with builders who value quality, so you'll seek them out at trade shows, gear your marketing materials to reflect the quality you provide, and have your business cards show your dedication to quality (no flimsy cards with perforated edges that you printed on your laser printer, for example).

Finally, knowing what your purpose is in your business, you create your goals. You might need a graphic designer to design your logo, rather than delegating that work to your nephew. You will need a professional website. You might need to establish relationships with specific vendors who carry the parts you like to use.

This story describes how your purpose informs every decision you make in your business. This is why it is so important to be clear about your purpose, and then make sure it shines through everything you do.

Look at the diagram and see how it reflects the purpose of our plumber, and how that purpose touches everything else in her business.

Everything is Connected

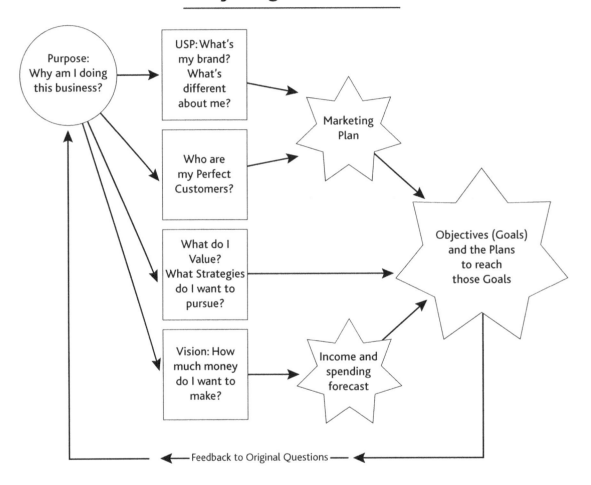

Copyright Clarity to Business, 2006

Capture Your Ideas Here

Fold down the corner of this page. If ideas are already coming to you as you've begun reading, record them here. As you go through the workbook, continue using this sheet to keep track of things you need to follow up on, thoughts that occur to you, and areas where you want to do more research.

IDEAS:

THINGS TO FOLLOW UP ON:

THINGS TO RESEARCH:

Why Are You In Business?

Y̶ou are about to begin Part One of the workbook. This is the "feel-good" section. This is the part where you get to think about your Purpose (both for your business and for yourself in the business); your Vision for your business over the next twelve months, and three years; your Mission (as I am defining Mission here it is what you do and who you serve); and your Values.

Don't be fooled by the fact that this is the feel-good section. It is one of, if not the most, important sections of this book. The truth is, the clearer your work is in these first modules, the easier it will be to create marketing activities that work; to understand deeply what motivates your clients; to clarify what makes you different from your competition; and very importantly, to figure out how much money your business needs to earn.

You will also return to these beginning modules when something happens that makes you question why you're doing your business. Your work here will remind you of your Purpose.

The first module in this section is called Purpose. It asks the questions: Why This Business? Why You? Why Now? You don't have to be intent on creating world peace or curing cancer.

In fact, your deepest purpose for your business may simply be to take the best care of your family that you can. No need for high-faluting answers to these questions. You just need to know what's true for you.

The second module is Vision. Where do you want your business to be in twelve months and three years? Creating a business plan is like building a road; you need to know where to build the road so it reaches the right destination. The vision for your business is the road's destination.

Mission is the third module. It asks: What do you do? Who do you serve (i.e., who are your best clients)? Throughout the workbook, the more specific you are, the better. This is a great place to practice being very specific. The goal here is to create a mission statement that allows your prospective clients to recognize themselves when they hear it. This is a no-jargon zone.

The last module in this section is the one in which you identify your Values. You will ask yourself what principles/ethics/ideology you use to make decisions, especially the difficult ones. If you're in business for yourself, you've probably already been faced with difficult decisions. This module is where you decide how to decide.

Even though this is the feel-good, dare I say, "woo-woo" section, don't take it lightly. The work you do here forms the foundation for the rest of the plan. Remember: everything is connected.

Purpose

WHY ARE YOU IN BUSINESS?

> Many persons have a wrong idea of what constitutes true happiness. It is not attained through self-gratification but through fidelity to a worthy purpose.
>
> **HELEN KELLER**

Being in business can be challenging and difficult, as well as deeply rewarding, both financially and personally. In times of challenge and difficulty, understanding why you went into business in the first place needs to be strong enough to carry you through. It's almost like being in a marriage—recalling why you decided to get married in the first place can carry you through the days when the going is rough.

Additionally, your reasons for going into business form the foundation of your brand: the personality of the business that shines through everything you do. Your business's purpose permeates your marketing materials, your website, the way you answer the phone, what you wear, and everything else that you tell people about your business.

The clearer you are about why you are in business, or why you want to start a business, the easier it is to communicate those reasons to your clients, employees, vendors and other stakeholders. When these groups are clear about your purpose, they can most effectively help you to succeed.

Finally, being clear about your purpose will help you set priorities, guide you in tackling any challenges, and help you make the right decisions.

Many businesses even have a story or an event that propelled them into starting a new venture. Did you wake up one morning and realize you could serve the clients better than your current employer was doing? Did you notice that the customers who patronized the business where you worked were asking repeatedly for services or products your employer wouldn't provide? Did your

Being clear about your purpose will help you set priorities, guide you in tackling any challenges, and help you make the right decisions.

neighbors frequently show up on the weekends asking you to help them do something or give them advice about something?

Is there a turning point in your life that propelled you into business for yourself? Think about this as you answer the questions on the following pages.

When you know why, you can always figure out how.

If you are working in a group, answer questions 1–4 below on your own, then find a partner and share your answers.

If you are working with a partner, answer questions 1–4 below, then share your answers with your partner.

If you are working alone, answer all the questions below.

1. Think about why your started your business, or want to start one. Consider these questions as you write the story of starting your business.

    *   Did something happen to propel you into business? What was it?

    *   What motivates you in your work?

    *   What innovations do you bring to your industry?

    *   What do you like about being your own boss?

    *   How are you doing a better job than other businesses already out there?

    *   How are you maximizing your talents and passions?

    *   Use the space below and the next page to briefly write the story of starting your business.

2. Now think about the reasons you have your business—freedom, passion, financial reward . . . ?

- Would you work in your business even if you weren't getting paid?
- What motivates you to do *this* business?
- How does this business help you live your purpose?
- Why it is critical *for you* that your business thrives?
- Why is it critical for the world for your business to thrive?
- What value do you create and deliver for your clients?
- What kinds of clients will benefit the most from working with you and your business?
- Will anyone else benefit from your business besides your clients and you? Who?

Use this space to make notes about the answers to the questions above:

3. Based on your answers to questions 1–2 above, list up to 5 reasons why you are in business (or more, if you have more):

1. _____

_____

2. _____

_____

3. _____

_____

4. _____

_____

5. _____

_____

4. Now return to the five reasons you wrote in question 3 and put them in order of your passion for each one. In other words, 1 is the reason you are most passionate about, and 5, the one you are least passionate about. Re-copy them in the space below:

1. _____

_____

2. _____

_____

3. _____

_____

4. _____

_____

5. _____

_____

5. Share the story of your business and your motivations with your group or your partner. If you are working alone, consider sharing the story of your business and your motivations to do it, with a friend. Take notes below of any feedback you receive. Does any of the feedback make you want to change your purpose? If so, go back to questions 3–4 and make those changes.

Copy the reasons you listed in question 4 above (up to five) to Section 1 of the *Passion, Plan, Profit* Business Plan Template on page 215.

Vision
THE DESTINY OF YOUR BUSINESS

> If one advances confidently in the direction of his dreams, and endeavors to live the life which he has imagined, he will meet with a success unexpected in common hours.
>
> HENRY DAVID THOREAU

You will start this module by establishing your revenue and salary visions. These numbers are crucial for two reasons:

- First, a business that is not profitable and does not produce an abundant living for its owner will close. You will lose the opportunity to do the work you were meant to do and your customers will miss experiencing your services and products.

- Second, you will use these revenue and salary numbers to determine the number of customers and clients your business needs in order to attain your revenue and salary goals.

Once you have determined your revenue and salary numbers, you will spend time considering other aspects of your business and what you want them to look like in the next 12 months, and in the next three years.

Before starting this, let's talk for a minute about money.

Almost everyone (okay, everyone) comes to adulthood with baggage, delusions, weird beliefs and downright craziness about money.

You might be getting angry right now, faced with the request I am making of you to identify how much money you want your business to make, and how much of that money you want to take home. Money may be a taboo subject for you. Or you might think it's dirty, or in bad taste to talk about it. Or you may think that wanting money makes you evil. After all, doesn't the Bible say that "money is the root of

all evil?" (The correct quote is actually "love of money is the root of all evil," which is a much different message.)

Or you might be afraid. "How am I supposed to know how much revenue I want to bring in this year? My business has only been going for six months (or maybe I haven't even started yet). Do I pull these numbers out of my nose?"

Or you might feel embarrassed. You might know exactly how much money you want to make, and it's a big number. What's more, you have a good shot at hitting your goal. What will people think? That you're greedy, or shallow, or a money-grubber?

Here's the truth. No matter how you feel about money, in order for your business to succeed, you must be clear about it. Vagueness around money is one of the primary reasons businesses fail. If you have already enjoyed the sheer agony of a failed business, you may have experienced this truth firsthand.

It's also important to know your goals, because once again, everything is connected. When you know what sales number you want to hit, you can calculate how many products you need to sell, or services you need to provide, to hit the target. Knowing the number of things you need to sell then connects you to the steps you need to take to reach enough people every month to hit those targets. If you need to fill 5 workshops per month with 10 people in each, you need to reach at least 50 people (probably more like 100+) to get 50 people to sign up.

I will admit it's more challenging to come up with a revenue and salary goal when you're just starting out. In that case, start with your living expenses (and not the version where you live in your car).

Multiply them by four (I know this may be a big number), and make that your revenue goal for the year. You can refine it later, when you get to the numbers module. The reason I tell you to multiply it by four is to cover these things: your business expenses, all taxes, a savings account for the inevitable rainy day in the business, retirement, and of course, your own salary.

If you're lucky and you've got a big revenue goal, and know you have a chance to hit it, *celebrate*! Think of all the good you can do with that money!

Ultimately, it doesn't matter how you feel about estimating your revenue; you just have to do it. If it causes you pain, fear, shame or other painful emotions, use those as an indicator that you need to do some work in this area. There are many great books on the subject of money. I have listed some of them in the Appendix. My primary message to you is: *don't let your baggage get in the way of your Vision and Purpose.* If you need to work on your beliefs about money, do it. There are vast resources to help with this. In the meantime, don't let your money luggage sabotage your business success.

Now, back to Visions. Here are some examples of visions from other small businesses:

> In 2021, Phoenix Carpet Cleaning/Restoration generates 5 million dollars in revenue. My (the owner's) take-home pay is $200,000. We open an office in Las Vegas and this office brings in 40% of our sales and profit by year-end 2022. Our whole business is computerized, and both offices are connected. We have a part-time bookkeeper on staff. The business has a savings account totaling six months of operating expenses in the bank. I spend two full days a week on marketing. We pick a charity for the year and donate 10% of our profit to them. All the employees have a vision for themselves and their progress in the company. We have yearly performance reviews. I am in the process of creating an employee stockownership program as part of the project to have the employees eventually own the business. I have fun every day at work.

See how this vision touches many aspects of this business; from operations, sales, technology, financial issues and human resources? Yours can do that too, but that isn't necessary.

Here is another example. This vision is more about how this company plans to spread the message of golf all over the world, and is less concerned with listing a litany of projects for the year:

> GolfTech web design generates $1 million in revenue in 2022. I take home $250,000 in salary. We are the one-stop shop for web development and search-engine marketing for golf courses, both in North America and across the world. We are considered the best

If you need to work on your beliefs about money, do it. There are vast resources to help with this. In the meantime, don't let your money luggage sabotage your business success.

web development company in the industry, and all the leaders come to us first. We hire only golf enthusiast employees and set aside one late afternoon a week for everyone to play at least 9 holes of golf. Our whole reason for being is to help our clients spread the joy of golf around the world.

As long as you start with the total revenue (revenue = sales) in your vision, and what part of that you plan to take home as your salary, the rest is fair game. You can make a list of projects you want to complete by the end of the coming year. Or you could do what GolfTech did, above, and talk more about the "feeling" of the company and how you want to be seen in the world. Or, you can do something in between or completely different.

You are building a road for your business to follow over the next twelve months. To build a road, you need to know where it's going. The Vision is your destination. It's the place you want to end up twelve months from now. The questions that follow will help you create your Vision, first for 12 months, then for 3 years from now.

The Vision is your destination. Your business plan is the road you're building to take you there.

If you are working in a group, answer questions 1, 2 and 3 below on your own, then find a partner and share your answers.

If you are working with a partner, answer questions 1, 2 and 3 below, then share your answers with your partner.

If you are working alone, answer questions 1–3 below. Then find someone to share your vision with (trusted advisor, coach, CPA, etc.).

1. Where do you want your business to be financially 12 months from today? How much revenue do you want to have generated in the next 12 months, and what do you want your gross salary to be before taxes?

    Total Revenue for the next 12 months: _____

    My Taxable Salary for the next 12 months: _____

2. Think about what you want the rest of your business to look like in 12 months. Some questions to ask yourself are:

    •   What do you want your office to look like?

    •   How many customers/clients do you want to have?

    •   What new systems do you want to have in place?

    •   What new technology do you want to invest in?

    •   What new employees do you want to hire?

    •   What new products do you want to sell?

    •   What new services do you want to provide?

Use the space below and on the next page to develop your one-year vision:

3. Imagine your business three years from now.

- How big will it be?
- How much revenue will you generate?
- How many employees will you have?
- Where will you be located?
- What will be different?
- What will you have learned?

Use the space below to develop your three-year vision:

4. Share your vision with someone in your group, your partner, or if you're working alone, with a trusted advisor. Take notes of any feedback you receive.

Copy the most important points from this module to Section 2 of the *Passion, Plan, Profit* Business Plan Template on page 215.

Mission
YOUR SERVICE TO THE WORLD

I say in speeches that a plausible mission of artists is to make people appreciate being alive at least a little bit. I am then asked if I know of any artists who pulled that off. I reply, "The Beatles did."

KURT VONNEGUT

There is an avalanche of books, blogs, Web sites, and other information about mission statements. An unsuspecting business owner could get confused trying to figure out what one is, let alone how to write one.

I'm going to simplify the process for you. This is all your mission statement needs to do:

1. Tell people what you do.
2. Describe your perfect clients.

Your mission statement will be simple and short, clear, and jargon-free.

It will also clearly identify your ideal customers so that they will recognize themselves when they read or hear it.

Let's start with how not to do it:

"Guided by relentless focus on our five imperatives, we will constantly strive to implement the critical initiatives required to achieve our vision. In doing this, we will deliver operational excellence in every corner of the Company and meet or exceed our commitments to the many constituencies we serve. All of our long-term strategies and short term actions will be molded by a set of core values that are shared by each and every associate."

Can you see what's wrong with this?

> Your mission statement will be simple and *short*, clear, and jargon-free. It will also clearly identify your ideal customers so that they will recognize themselves when they read or hear it.

What they do, and who they do it for, are missing in action. What does this business do, exactly? Who are their "many constituencies?" How much did they pay someone to write this?

This is a real, live mission statement for a chain of nationwide grocery stores, but you wouldn't know that, since they neglected to mention what business they were actually in. You can do better.

Here are some more compelling examples from large companies:

Yahoo!: *To connect people to their passions, communities, and the world's knowledge.*

This is pretty good. It's short and jargon-free. We get what they do (connect people to their passions, communities, and the world's knowledge); and we get who they do it for (people). I would argue that their audience is not all people, but maybe they would argue back.

Here is Google's mission statement: *To organize the world's information and make it universally accessible and useful.*

This one is good too, although it doesn't say who they're doing the organizing for. Maybe they're like Yahoo!, they want to do this for everyone.

Here are some other good ones:

Kraft Foods: *Helping People Around the World Eat and Live Better.*

H&R Block: *To help our clients achieve their financial objectives by serving as their tax and financial partner.*

Here's an ambitious mission statement from Darden Restaurants: *We take pride in providing a terrific dining experience to every guest, every time, in every one of our restaurants. That is how we will be the best company in casual dining, now and for generations.*

HotJobs: *Our mission is to be essential to jobseekers by helping them advance their careers, and employers by helping them build their workforce.*

CVS: *We will be the easiest pharmacy retailer for customers to use.*

McGraw Hill: *Our mission is to provide essential information and insight that help individuals, markets and societies perform to their potential.*

Here are some Mission Statement examples from (real) small businesses:

Williams Financial helps families plan for a secure financial future for themselves and their special-needs children.

Phoenix Carpet Cleaning provides "green" carpet cleaning services to environmentally conscious, discriminating homeowners and their offices.

Susan Thomas Associates, an international software consulting firm, helps the Fortune 100 and large governmental agencies manage, collaborate with and control their documents using Adobe software solutions.

JD Computing provides first-quality computer products and services to businesses that value stability and doing things right the first time.

Murphy Feldenkrais Practice provides healing and hope through classes, Feldenkrais Instruction, packages and instructional CDs, to people with serious neurological and physical challenges, and their families and caregivers.

Truthfully, I think the ones listed above are better than most of the ones from the Fortune 500 companies. Of course, I'm prejudiced. I was teaching a workshop once, and after I read the mission statement for Williams Financial, a woman in the workshop stopped me midsentence and said: "I need their telephone number. I've got to call them."

This is exactly what you want to happen when you tell someone (who is your perfect customer) your mission statement. You want them to get a wild look in their eye and demand your phone number.

Creating a mission statement can be challenging. Business people tend to list the features of their products, rather than the benefits the client receives. Williams Financial could have said "We invest money in the stock and bond markets for families with special needs children," but that statement is much less resonant. Why? Because it doesn't tell the perfect client what *benefit* they receive from investing their money in the stock and bond markets.

Don't worry if you don't come up with the perfect mission statement the first time. Also don't worry if it doesn't sound like it was crafted by a copywriter. Prospective clients will respond better to a mission statement that cites benefits they care about, than they will respond to something that is well written, but doesn't state the benefits.

On page 24, I have given you a template to create your first mission statement. Take a look at it now to see what you're shooting for. After you answer the questions below, use the template to take a stab at what you think your mission statement should be.

A mission statement crafted using this template, that specifically names your perfect customers and clearly states the benefits to them of working with you, is perfectly fine. Your customers will sense your sincerity and intention through a not-so-perfect mission statement. If you can hone it further, so much the better.

Also, this is a place where input from other people is very useful. If you're working alone, corner someone (one of your perfect customers, if you have one) and run your efforts by them. You will be able to tell when you hit upon the mission statement that is right for you; it will resonate when you say it out loud.

When you can clearly tell people what you do and who you do it for, your perfect clients will recognize you as the person they must hire to solve their problems.

If you are working in a group, answer questions 1–9 below on your own, then find a partner and share your answers. After you have received feedback from each other, create a mission statement by yourself using the templates on pages 24–25. If you're feeling really inspired, try editing it using the space on page 26.

When you are finished, share your final effort with the group and get their feedback. It's crucial to make sure they "get" what you do. If in doubt, get them to explain it back to you, using different words. Edit your mission statement using their feedback, until you are satisfied your perfect customers will recognize that your business is the one they've been searching for, when they hear it.

If you are working with a partner, answer questions 1–9 below, and then share your answers with your partner. After you have received feedback from each other, create a mission statement using the templates on pages 24–25. If you're feeling really inspired, try editing it using the space on page 26.

When you are finished, share your final effort with your partner and get their feedback. It's crucial to make sure your partner "gets" what you do. If in doubt, get him or her to explain it back to you, using different words. Edit your mission statement using his/her feedback, until you are satisfied your perfect customers will recognize that your business is the one they've been searching for, when they hear it.

If you are working alone, answer questions 1–6 below. Do the work on pages 24–25 to create your statement. If possible, run it by some of your best clients to get their feedback. If you're feeling really inspired, try editing it using the space on page 26.

Before beginning, review the mission statement template (on page 24) one more time to understand the end result you are striving for.

1   What does your business do?

2.   What problems does your business solve, or what pain does it alleviate for your customers?

3.   What do your clients really buy from you? (In the case of a computer vendor, clients may really buy peace of mind and reliability as much as the actual PC or service itself). Are your clients buying something more than a product or service? If so, what is that "something more?" What are the benefits you provide to them?

4. What reach do you want to have?

   - Local?

   - Regional?

   - National?

   - International?

5. What businesses do you most want to be like? Why? (Note: you can admire or want to be like a business that does the same work as yours does, or you can admire a business that is completely different. Perhaps a business you think highly of has outstanding customer service, or is in a great location, or has systemized all their processes so everything runs smoothly. If you're having trouble thinking of a business you like, think about where you spend your own money.)

Business name	Characteristics you admire about them

6. What are some of the characteristics of the customers you are most successful in selling your goods and services to (i.e., are they families, business people, homeowners in a certain zip code, people with specific health issues, construction businesses?) List the characteristics of your best clients below:

From the answers to the questions above, make three attempts at writing your Mission Statement using the templates below.

See page 19 again for examples.

Attempt #1:

_____(name of business), a _____

_____(what area: local, regional, national, etc.)

_____(what type of business) provides

_____(type of goods/services) to

_____(what kind of customers).

Attempt #2:

Name of your business _____

What it does _____

Who it does this work for (i.e., what kind of customers?):

_____

Attempt #3:

Name of your business _____

What it does _____

Who it does this work for (i.e., what kind of customers?):

_____

Note: Thanks to Jim Horan and The One Page Business Plan who inspired this template.

Another example:

> SuperCleaners (name of your business) thoroughly and mindfully cleans the homes and offices (what your business does) of discerning, environmentally-conscious clients in the Phoenix Metro area (who you do this work for).

When you have a working mission statement, transfer it to Section 3 of the *Passion, Plan, Profit* Business Plan Template on page 215.

Now you're going to take your mission statement from the template above and attempt to distill it into eight words (or so).

The reason to try this is that sometimes a very resonant and memorable mission statement that doesn't follow the formula can be distilled from the formulaic one. Here's an example:

Formulaic Mission Statement: "Cambridge Investment Research, an international financial firm, provides financial advice and consulting to high-net-worth individuals, to help them create a secure financial future."

Distilled Mission Statement: "Cambridge Investment Research matches exceptional investors with exceptional investments."

You can see that the second mission statement "sings," as compared with the first.

Outside the confines of the formula above, make three attempts to distill into 8 words, each time, what your business does, and for whom. The point of this is to hone the message into something sleeker, more streamlined and resonant. This will also give you practice in getting to the essence of what your business actually does.

Attempt #1 _____

_____

Attempt #2 _____

_____

Attempt #3 _____

_____

If you come up with a distilled mission statement that you like, show it to your group if you're working in a group, to your partner if you're working on this together, or a client/your CPA/your coach or other trusted advisor if you're working alone. See if they agree that it describes the essence of what you do and who you do it for. If it's better than the formulaic one, substitute this one for your original mission statement.

Values
YOUR MORAL COMPASS

Your beliefs become your thoughts. Your thoughts become your
words. Your words become your actions. Your actions become
your habits. Your habits become your values. Your values become
your destiny.

MAHATMA GANDHI

Your values are who you are in the world; your philosophy of
business. The list may not be long, but it can be deeply meaningful.

Your values are the principles you will use when faced with difficult,
morally ambiguous decisions. Deeply-considered values will rescue
you when you don't know what to do. If you pick the right values, they
will stay the same no matter what business you're in.

When you're not sure what to do and you haven't clarified your
values so they can guide you through a sticky situation, bad things can
happen. You can get talked into doing something you know isn't
right. You might make a decision based strictly on logic or strictly
on economics, or money, or emotion.

Knowing your values will allow you to make the right decisions
under pressure. When you know your values ahead of time, you can
make the right call without having to succumb to the latest worry or
whim, or outside influence.

I guarantee you that every business, and every business owner, will
face morally ambiguous decisions, and not just once or twice a year.
They most commonly arise when there is a conflict between doing the
right thing and earning more money.

For example, say one of your values is one I have listed below:
The Right Fit. This means you do business with people who are the
right fit for your services, and you send those who aren't the right fit
to other companies.

> Knowing your values
> will allow you to
> make the right
> decisions under
> pressure. When you
> know your values
> ahead of time, you
> can make the right
> call without having
> to succumb to the
> latest worry or
> whim, or outside
> influence.

Someday, a wealthy potential client will walk in your door who is not a great fit, and you're going to want to say yes. This is when your values come to the rescue. The reason you have this value in the first place is because you already have experience doing business with clients who weren't the right fit, resulting in pain and suffering for everyone. Knowing and acting on your value of "The Right Fit" will save you from experiencing further pain.

Interestingly, like everything else in life, your most effective values will be the ones you learn from making painful mistakes. I once took on a client that I knew was a bad fit and it cost my company (i.e., me) $5,000. Not huge money, but enough to sear the lesson into my brain.

One of the more famous corporate values is Google's "Don't be evil." This value is portable; it would work for Google no matter what product or service they decided to offer. It also provides guidance in making decisions in any area of the business: from hiring, to new product development, to vendor and competitor relations.

A local marketing firm in Arizona says "We're nice people and we only do business with nice people." This value also provides guidance across many areas of the business. It helps the firm choose which clients to do business with, which employees to hire, and which vendors to use. It can even guide the firm in the kinds of marketing it recommends to its clients.

Identified correctly, your values will help you create your "business personality," also known as your brand. Your brand communicates what every interaction will be like between your business and everyone it touches: clients, vendors, employees, and other stakeholders.

Here are some possible values to consider:

- Integrity
- Financial responsibility
- Respect for the individual
- The right fit
- Clarity
- Employees first
- Clients first
- Reputation first

- No disparagement of competition

- Honesty

- Open-mindedness

- Transparency

- Hard work

- Balance

- Success

- Green (environmental awareness in all its forms)

You can see that some of these very worthy values contradict each other. Do your clients come first, or do your employees? Whom do you stand behind in a dispute between a client and an employee? Do you guard your reputation above everything, or must you be transparent about your numbers, your policies, and your mistakes (as many public companies must)? Do you promote balance: no overtime, family comes first; or success: no matter what it takes we'll deliver what we said? If success is a value, how do you define it?

The answers you give to these questions below will begin to create the framework for marketing, inform how your business will sell to prospects, serve your clients, set prices, handle disputes, hire and fire employees, choose new clients, keep existing clients, even what your business cards, website and stationery will look like. You are already running your life (and possibly your business) using a set of values. This is the time to make them conscious.

Honoring your own values will keep you out of expensive, embarrassing trouble.

If you are working in a group, select another partner (preferably someone you haven't worked with yet), and interview each other, answering questions 1–7 below. Copy your partner's answers into the pages below, and have him/her do the same for you.

If you are working with a partner, interview each other, answering questions 1–7 below. Copy your partner's answers into the pages below, and have him/her do the same for you.

If you are working alone, answer questions 1–7 below.

1. What company or companies would you like to model your business after? What values do they hold that make them attractive to you?

Company	Value(s)

2. What companies would you NOT model your business after? Why not? Knowing what you don't want can help you identify what you do want. Is there anything that a company is doing that you can't stand?

Company	What you don't like about them

3. List 2–5 rules that you use to make decisions in your business now. Here are some examples: We don't work with anyone involved with pornography. We make sure all our employees are legal immigrants. We hire undocumented workers and help them get legal. We don't take any jobs below X% profit. We tithe 10% of every job to charity. Review the list of values on pages 28–29 for more suggestions of values you may already be using.

1.

2.

3.

4.

5.

4. Think about some clients you didn't do business with (or wished you hadn't) because they didn't fit. What characteristic(s) of those clients made you back away?

5. List a few ways your vendors and/or subcontractors would like you to treat them:

6. List a few ways your employees (if you have them) would like you to treat them:

7. Look over the answers to these questions and glean from them 3–5 values that you will use (or are already using) to run your business.

1.

2.

3.

4.

5.

Once you have a set of core values, transfer them to Section 4 of the *Passion, Plan, Profit* Business Plan Template on page 215.

How Are You In Business?

Now that you know the Purpose of your business, your Vision for the next twelve months and three years, your Mission and your Values, it's time to look closer. The modules in the next section get more specific and practical.

You're going to figure out who your best customers are (your People), what's different about you and your company compared to your competitors, what's going on in the marketplace, and how you want to present your company to the outside world.

The first module in this section takes you through figuring out who your People are; those folks most in need of what you sell, who can—and are happy to—pay your prices. This is the longest module in the section, so take your time. I started this section with the People module, because once you know who you most want to work with, it will help you answer some of the questions in the subsequent sections.

The next module is Strategies. I spend a lot of time in this module defining what strategies are, because the term can be confusing.

One way to look at strategies is just to think of them as the rules you use to design how your company works and to market your products and services.

For example, if one of your strategies is to educate your People (as mine is), then all your marketing has to educate, in addition to encouraging people to buy. If your strategy is to make sure you never have to go back and fix something twice (i.e., No Rework), then you design the company (with standards, extra training, sophisticated support structure, etc.) so that when a technician goes out to the field, he has the training and support to fix the problem the first time. Answering the questions in the second module will lead you to your strategies.

The third module will help you figure out your Unique Selling Proposition (abbreviated, USP). This concept was invented in the 1960s by a marketing genius named Rosser Reeves. To succeed, he said, companies had to figure out what was different about their product(s) compared to every similar product on the market. When the first edition of this book came out, Reeves' book, *Reality in Advertising*, was out of print. That problem has been rectified. You can now buy a Kindle version for $8.00.

Whether you buy a copy of his book or not, you can still figure out what you do better than anyone else. This module will help. If you already have a business that is serving the people you want to reach, you can get them to help you figure out what's different about you.

The final module in this section is the Strengths, Weaknesses, Opportunities, and Threats (often abbreviated, "SWOT"). The work in this module will help you look at your marketplace and your competition. It can be challenging and sometimes scary to look at what the competition is doing, but because the universe is abundant (and if you don't believe me, go to the drugstore and look at how many different kinds of toothpaste are on sale), you don't need to worry about the competition. You just need to learn from them. It's especially important to look closely at the competitors who are serving the same People you are, so you can see what's working and what isn't. When you finish these modules, you'll be more than halfway through. Keep Going!

Target Marketing
FIND YOUR PEOPLE, MAKE RELATIONSHIPS WITH THEM, HELP THEM BUY

A Perfect Customer is one whose needs are a perfect fit for a company's mission.

STACEY HALL AND JAN BROGNIEZ:
ATTRACTING PERFECT CUSTOMERS

When I wrote this chapter the first time in 2009, I used business language to describe the people who need your work. I called them your "Target Market." Experience has shown me I attract many more people in my 'target market" when I start by visualizing them as people instead of targets or markets. I like to think about them being different groups of fellow humans who need my help, and that I've got the perfect training plus experience to help them. I (or my business and I) do something or make something really well, and my people need whatever this is.

Your job then, is to figure out who these people are for your business, where to find them; make relationships with them, and help them buy.

Let's start with who they are.

Many business owners think that a bigger group of people to sell to will guarantee a more successful business. The more people who need your product, the more you'll sell. So, let's appeal to the largest group of people possible. Seems obvious.

But it's wrong.

Take the example of a product that every human being must have, and at least three times a day, no less: food. Does that mean everyone on the planet is a potential customer for the corner convenience store, or the local farmer's market, or a bigger grocery store or a big-box store like Target or Wal-Mart? It's possible you've shopped at all these places at least once, but I'll bet one or two of them are the places you do 90%

of your food shopping. Additionally, you'd be irritated if someone made you shop at one of the food stores you don't like. Why? Because you're not their people.

Can you imagine the generic marketing a grocery store might do if they thought they could attract a larger group of customers by being less specific (and therefore more attractive to more people)? "We sell food." That marketing message is true, general, broad and theoretically appealing to all of us since we all need food. It's also boring, vague and virtually useless. What kind of food? Canned? Fresh? Asian? Pre-packaged, local, imported, expensive, lowest price? Are you down the street or do I have to drive 20 miles out of town? Is the store clean? Do you carry meat or are you a produce market? As the marketing gets more specific more people are weeded out, but the ones left are the true fans who want more than just "food," who will come back week after week.

Your job is to get as precise and detailed as possible about the group of humans you want to work with, so when you describe what you do and who you help, your people will recognize that you understand them and their problems and you're the best solution for them.

In 2009, finding information beyond the basics about your humans was difficult and expensive. Social media has revolutionized this process.

Then, as now, you needed to know who your people were on the outside and the inside. This information was broken into "inside" and "outside" categories because the outside information (aka 'demographic' information) was cheap and easy to find. Outside information included details like age, sex, race, education, family size, number of children, address; the US Census collected this data, made it public, and data aggregation companies sold it cheaply.

Who people are on the inside; their interests, hobbies, values, political affiliation or lack thereof, where they liked to travel, what they read, what they watched, what they bought, (called "psychographic" information) was not.

Imagine: people used to call us (on our land lines!) and ask us about our values and habits, and we often answered their questions. We filled out "warranty postcards" that came with kitchen appliances that asked a host of questions unrelated to the appliance, thinking that the warranty wouldn't be valid if we didn't hand over this information. Then some poor person, locked in a windowless office whose grey walls were lined with motivational posters, had to key all this information into a database.

Only companies with giant marketing budgets could afford to conduct these surveys or buy the information from other companies because it was so labor-intensive and expensive to collect.

Not anymore.

Don't worry, though. If you are allergic to social media, you don't have to use it. There are other ways to find your people. However, social media makes it so easy to find the people you want to work with, it's like trying to pass up a giant plate of warm chocolate chip cookies every time you're hungry.

Social media does make it easy to find people. But you still have to understand and be able to describe who you want to find. We'll start there, then move on to where you will find them, how you'll make relationships with them, and how you'll help them buy.

If you are working in a group, select another partner (preferably someone you haven't worked with yet), and interview each other, answering questions 1-5 below. Copy your partner's answers into his book and have him/her do the same for you.

If you are working with a partner, interview each other, answering questions 1-5 below. Copy your partner's answers into the book, and have him/her do the same for you.

If you are working alone, answer questions 1-5 below.

For everyone: once you've finished answering questions 1-5, fill out the grid on page 55 on your own.

1. Think about your best clients and what inner and outer characteristics they have in common. If you don't have any clients or customers yet, imagine the characteristics of the clients you'd most like to work with. I've listed some possible characteristics of consumers first, then characteristics of businesses, depending on who you sell to. Don't skip over one list for the other. Businesses almost always reflect the values of their owners; even though it might not make sense to think about the political affiliation of a business for instance, the owners may care about politics in a way that influences how or if you work with the business itself. Business characteristics might be relevant for your consumers also.

Possible characteristics of consumers:

*   The obvious outside information about them: age, sex, race, location, education, family size, number of children, marital status.

*   How much money they have.

*   Their political affiliation.

*   How they respond to change.

*   Their personal values.

*   What they do in their leisure time.

- How technical they are (or aren't).

- How creative they are/how creative they want you to be.

Possible characteristics of businesses:

- The obvious outside information about them: type of business, size, location, number of employees, years in business, number of customers.

- Who *their* clients are.

- How profitable they are.

- How often they need your products/services.

- Their business values.

- Their mission.

- I saw a sign at a cabinet shop once that said: "Fast, cheap, good. Pick two." Which do your clients value most highly? Is it so important to be one of these that the other two don't matter?

And for both:

- Their top sources of pain (that you can relieve).

Because knowing (or imagining) as much detail as possible about who your clients are, I'm going to have you fill out those characteristics in the table below. To simplify the worksheet shuffling, choose a name for each type of client you're describing, and copy that name into the table on page 55, along with the other information you'll put together about where to find your clients, make relationships with them, and help them buy.

You will probably have or want more than one type of client. Maybe one is your group of new clients just beginning to work with you, while two other groups have been with you longer. Or three different kinds of customers use three subsets of your products, and their characteristics differ enough that you'd talk to them differently. If they are different enough from each other, describe them separately. I've given you space to describe five types of clients. There's nothing magic about the number five; it's just that marketing to more than that is too hard for most small businesses.

Before you fill out this table, also spend a few minutes thinking about the characteristics of your worst clients (past, present or imaginary). For instance, even though I often work with clients who aren't yet making money in their businesses, I still want ones who pay their bills within the terms we agreed upon. If people need payment plans I'm fine negotiating them, but once we've agreed on the terms that work for both of us, I want the kind of clients who stick to what we negotiated. I also don't like working with people who come late to coaching sessions. So "clients who show up on time and who pay their bills as agreed" are two important characteristics of people I want to work with. Sometimes it's easier to visualize what you do want by understanding first what you don't want.

Here's the description of one type of customer for a pizzeria that sells pizza made with organic ingredients that are locally sourced:

Client Type	Description: everything you know about who they are on the inside and the outside.
Pizza Family	Families within a 7 mile radius with at least one child under 18, with an income range of $50K-$100K where both parents are employed, who care about the quality of the food they eat but don't have time to cook, who shop at the neighborhood farmers' market, who like having their kids' friends over for parties and sleep-overs, who recycle, and compost food waste.

Here's a possible client description for an artist:

Client Type	Description: everything you know about who they are on the inside and the outside.
First home as an adult	Singles and couples between the ages of 24-35, attended some college or graduated, first-time homebuyers, like vintage home furnishings, live within a 5 mile radius of the city center, who eat at locally-owned restaurants in their area, who 'like' local businesses and artists on Facebook/Instagram who want to furnish their homes with original art.

Or for a CPA:

Client Type	Description: everything you know about who they are on the inside and the outside.
Family business, complex tax situation	Own or partner in a family business with revenues of $10 mil-$50 mil with multiple locations in different states with different tax laws; numerous family members also partners in the business who get along with each other, using a robust accounting software package and are meticulous in their accounting.

Or for a life coach:

Client Type	Description: everything you know about who they are on the inside and the outside.
Empty-nest women who want to re-enter the workforce	Women aged 45-55, have at least one child of college age, income of $50K+, not been employed outside the home for the past 10 years, in a partnership, some college or college graduate, technically savvy, active at their children's school, volunteer experience with non-profits.

1. Now that you know what you want and what you don't, describe your perfect customer(s) here:

Client Type	Description: everything you know about who they are on the inside and the outside.
1.	
2.	
3.	
4	
5.	

For questions 2-4 we will gather more information to complete the grid on page 55.

2. Now that you know what your perfect customers look like, where would you find them? You have two broad choices: on or off the Internet (or both, of course). Here are some places you might find your customers in real life:

   - Leads or networking groups like BNI, trade associations, or your local Chamber of Commerce.

   - Referrals from other people you do business with, like your CPA, landlord, bank or vendors. You might create a group of referral partners who refer business to each other, especially when you all need to work closely together on a joint outcome for a single client. Wedding planners, photographers, florists, venues and caterers are the perfect example of a referral partnership group, as are general contractors and their subs.

   - Church, social clubs, Meet-Ups, Toastmasters, Rotary, Kiwanis.

   - A mailing list (yes, you can still buy these) that includes everyone within a specific radius of your business, and/or that meet certain criteria like type of business or household they are, number of employees or family members, etc.

   - And the gold standard: referrals from existing clients.

If you want to find your clients on the internet, go where they are. For the next five minutes or until something changes again, more "business-y" businesses find their clients on LinkedIn, and more consumer-oriented businesses find theirs on Facebook, Instagram, SnapChat, Pinterest, Yelp, TripAdvisor, and now TikTok. There are also many other smaller social media platforms, but it's more important to pick one that seems right, create a profile and start interacting than to obsess much about picking the right one (although if you're a CPA, unless you are the CPA to teenage video stars, skip TikTok). If you don't know which one to pick, look up your competitors and see what they're doing. It's important to pick the right platform, but it's much more crucial to get on it and start making friends.

The way social media platforms work is that you create a profile for your business, invite people to come to your profile and follow you, then interact with them in a meaningful way so they invite more people. Once you have even 100 followers, you can buy advertising from the social media platform that targets people who don't know about you yet, but who match the profile of the people who already do.

This is the scary magic of social media, and why no one cares anymore about demographic information being cheaper or easier to get than psychographic. Once you have a hundred fans interacting with you, the social media company can present your information to an almost unlimited number of new people who MATCH the fans you already have.

Here are some examples of where the businesses listed above might start looking for their people.

For the pizzeria:

Customer	Where to find them
Pizza family	Buy a mailing list from VistaPrint or InfoUSA or other mailing list broker, of families who fit this criteria and mail coupons. "Claim" the business on Yelp and Trip Advisor (put up a profile on the site with photos and ask customers to review you). Interact with your reviewers. Set up a Facebook page and ask your personal friends to 'like' your pizzeria, Once you get customers, ask them to like the page, then post information every day that would make your existing customers want to share it with their friends.

For the visual artist:

Customer	Where to find them
First home as an adult	Find and join Facebook groups that support first time homebuyers. Join Instagram, post your art and follow people who look like the people you want to work with. See if there are Meet-ups in your area that focus on art appreciation, studio tours or other art-related activities and go to them, go to social events that your people might go to (concerts, art openings, new restaurant openings) and talk to people.

For the CPA:

Customer	Where to find them
Family business part-nership	Introduce yourself and be helpful to people already doing business with these clients: estate and business attorneys, financial advisors, insurance agents, even other CPAs who might not do this kind of work. Join the trade association that your clients would belong to. Find and join groups on LinkedIn that discuss these issues.

For the life coach:

Customer	Where to find them
Empty-nest woman	Find and join Facebook groups that support empty-nest women. Join Instagram and find other people posting about this subject, see if there is a website or Meet-Up group of mothers in your area, if you attend a church and it has a group for mothers, join it.

Once you've figured out where to find your people, turn to page 55 and fill in the second column in the table. If you have more than one type of client; list each one if you'd find them in different places. You're building the marketing portion of your business plan here.

3. Once you know where to look for your clients, what is the best way to engage, to get permission from your people to market to them? Here are some suggestions for on-and offline activities.

   Offline:

   - Joining a networking group or a trade association and actually showing for the meetings, volunteering on a committee, engaging with the other members and demonstrating your dependability and responsibility. Joining a group may be the first step in finding your people but it's not sufficient by itself. You have to make relationships.

   - Getting referrals from other people. These can come from existing clients, from other businesses who work with your clients but aren't your competitors (the wedding planner example), or even from competitors who don't offer something that their clients need. Same rule applies here. Getting referrals from people requires building relationships.

   In fact, if you're finding your clients offline, now that you've found them your whole job is to build relationships with them.

If you use social media to find your people online, the process of making relationships with them sometimes takes longer. Meeting people in person or on the phone is more like, well, meeting them. You see who they are in real life, you can have live interactions with them and it's much faster to see if you are a fit for what they need. On social media, it's possible to interact with a hundred different people in a day, but not make much of an impression on any of them. That's why the process of making relationships online can take longer.

Let's look at our same examples from above and see ways these different businesses could interact with their prospective clients, to make relationships with them.

For the pizzeria:

Client type	How to make relationships with them
Pizzeria family	Send regular coupons so they know you exist, once they become customers, ask for their email and permission to send them information about coupons and specials, be helpful: sponsor kids' sports teams, donate food to PTO meetings at the local elementary school, make a Facebook page and post information about making pizza, why yours is so good, what it's like to own a restaurant; in general, post information that's helpful to customers and also helps them see you as a person and part of the community. Once you gain your 100 followers you can start advertising to other people who match your followers' interests.

For the visual artist:

Client type	How to make relationships with them
First home as an adult	Interact! Once you've followed 100 people or so, (and even before that), comment on their feeds, offer helpful tips, (beyond just 'liking' their posts or commenting with an emoji). Be a real person; post photos of yourself (in moderation) and talk about your creative process. Respond quickly when people comment on your posts or send your direct messages. Once you have 100+ followers you can start advertising to people who match your followers' interests and ask them to join your email list. Email your people your helpful information about how to choose art for their home.

For the CPA:

Client type	How to make relationships with them
Small business owners with complex tax situations who need a financial plan.	Demonstrate your expertise through giving talks, blogging and putting up instructional videos on your website, joining and actually participating in associations where your referral sources also hang out, posting updates on new laws on your LinkedIn page. Get permission from existing clients to email them with updates and new information, then doing that consistently. Make sure your website is professional and up-to-date.

For the life coach:

Client type	How to make relationships with them
Empty-nest woman	Be a real person who interacts with other people and who posts information that's helpful, timely and relevant to your clients, and do it consistently. Make it easy to sign up for your email list, then email helpful information. Offer short discovery sessions (15 minutes) for people to brainstorm a problem with you for free.

As you think about how to make relationships with your clients, also consider what your competitors do. What's already working for them that you could emulate?

Also, don't forget that part of your relationship-building work needs to happen with existing clients. It's significantly more expensive to find new people for your practice than it is to earn repeat business from existing clients. You could make a case that 50% of your marketing money and time should be spent strengthening your existing relationships. I'm not sure what the right percentage is for you. I just want you to remember how easy it is to take your best clients for granted. You've undoubtedly been on the other end of this problem as a customer yourself and you know how disappointing it feels.

You'd be right if you noticed a theme among all the possible ways to make relationships with your people. Here it is: Get permission to talk to them (as opposed to bombarding them with messages they don't need or want), then be helpful, be human, be concise (don't waste their time), and be consistent. This idea of asking permission before communicating with your people was pioneered by Seth Godin in his book, *Permission Marketing*, over twenty years ago. At the time it was radical. Now we see it's simple, common courtesy, plus it's the only way to market that small businesses can afford. And ironically, it works better than any other kind of marketing.

Three more factors to consider when you're deciding how to make relationships with your people.

First, the way you decide to make relationships with your people needs to fit your personality, especially when you're starting out in business and you are your own 'making relationships' (i.e. marketing) department. One of the primary reasons marketing fails is that businesses don't do it consistently, and I guarantee you won't do your relationship building if you don't enjoy the way you picked to do it. If you think you should be networking and meeting lots of new people and you don't actually enjoy that, don't set yourself up for failure. You might be able to guilt yourself into doing it for a couple weeks but having to do something you dislike isn't sustainable. There are fifty ways to make relationships with your people. One or two of them will fit your personality nicely.

Next, the way you decide to make relationships with your people has to be congruent with your business. Real estate agents might post their vacation photos on their business Facebook page, but gastroenterologists must not. If you are the CPA to TikTok video stars you might have a TikTok profile, but for 99.9% of all profes-

SECTION 2

PASSION, PLAN, PROFIT

52

sional businesses like doctors, attorneys, CPAs, financial planners, having a TikTok profile at all, let alone posting to it, would damage relationships with their people rather than help.

Finally, when you make relationships with your people, consider who owns the information about them. The enormous downside of social media is that they own the information about your people, not you. Optimally, you ask permission from your people to market to them, they give you their email address or phone number, and you are the custodian of that information, not a social media company. That way when Facebook or whomever decides to limit your access to your people by charging you more money to talk to them, it won't matter so much. Using Facebook and other social media platforms to find your people and make relationships with them starts out being free. It costs nothing to set up a profile and begin conversing. Rapidly, however, if you want to continue to reach your fans, you have to pay. The best way to use social media is to find new people, then direct them to your website where they can opt in to regular communication from you (like emails or texts). Then when the social media company decides to change the rules (which is a given), you won't be hurt.

Unless you won the lottery (in which case you aren't reading this book anyway), you probably won't have an unending supply of money to spend on your marketing. Nevertheless, before you finalize how to find clients, make relationships and help them buy, it's useful to understand (or imagine) how much money you think a client will spend with you over the lifetime of your relationship with them. You want to know or estimate this figure because it can't cost more to get a client than the client will spend with you during your relationship with them. If it costs $1,000 to attract one client and they spend $900 with you before they move on, you'll lose $100 every time you get a new client and you'll run out of lottery money fast.

Admittedly, this is hard to calculate. The scientific wild-ass guess way is to add up all the money you spent on marketing and all your other business expenses in a year and divide it by the number of clients you had during that year. Then add up all your sales, divide that by the number of clients, and compare the two numbers. If the per-client expense amount is larger than the per-client sales amount, that's not good. Because you have to pay such close attention to money when you have a small business or solo practice usually this problem becomes obvious long before you've stopped to do any calculations, because you'll notice you aren't able to pay the bills. Just keep this in mind when you're figuring out your marketing.

Considering all these factors: fitness for your business, congruence with your personality, who owns the data, how much money you have to spend, and what kind of relationship building appeals to your people, fill in how you want to make relationships with them in the table on page 55.

4. Your final job is to make it easy for your people to buy from you. The rules are the same for every business, unless you're selling the Hope diamond. The less effort, the fewer clicks, the more streamlined your buying process is, the better. Don't spend all your time cultivating relationships, then when people want to buy from you, drop the ball by not answering the phone, or having difficult to find or broken links on your website, or making people direct message you to find out your prices or even to find out what you actually sell. They'll give up.

There are numerous, inexpensive apps you can use to help people buy from you. Two examples are Shopify and Big Cartel. They provide shopping carts you can use on your website or even with your Facebook page or Instagram feed and require no software coding or special technical ability. Many website template companies like Wix, Weebly or Squarespace provide the ability for your customers to buy directly from your website. This is not a comprehensive list; I've just named these few options to illustrate that you have plentiful alternatives to make it easy for your customers to order and buy from you. Don't skip this crucial step in your marketing or all your hard work to find your clients and make relationships with them will be wasted. Technology changes at the speed of light; before you pay money to any of these software companies I've listed, turn to the Resource section on page 225 and research who the best companies are right now.

Fill in the final column in the template below with the way(s) you will make it easy for your customers to buy from you.

MARKETING PLAN

This is the blueprint you'll use to help your people find you, how you'll make relationships with them, and how you'll help them buy.

Client type	Description	How to find them	How to make relationships with them	How to help them buy

Show this to someone (the person you're working with in your group, your partner if you were doing the work with someone else, or a trusted advisor if you're working alone). Get their feedback and make adjustments if necessary.

Once you are satisfied with this work on your people, transfer the information to section 5 of the Passion Plan Profit Business Plan Template on page 215.

Strategies
YOUR BUSINESS COMPASS

Strategic management is an ongoing process that assesses the business and the industries in which the company is involved; assesses its competitors and sets goals and strategies to meet all existing and potential competitors; and then reassesses each strategy annually or quarterly [i.e., regularly] to determine how it has been implemented and whether it has succeeded or needs replacement by a new strategy to meet changed circumstances, new technology, new competitors, a new economic environment, or a new social, financial, or political environment.

ROBERT BOYDEN LAMB

Strategy refers to how a company competes in a particular business. (Note: overall strategy for diversified firms is referred to as corporate strategy.) Competitive strategy is concerned with how a company can gain a competitive advantage through a distinctive way of competing.

INSTITUTE FOR STRATEGY AND COMPETITIVENESS, HARVARD BUSINESS SCHOOL

Strategy is like brilliance or artistic talent: it's difficult to define, but you know it when you see it. Even great business minds like the ones I quoted above (Robert Lamb wrote a textbook on business strategy, and we all know how smart the people are at the Harvard Business School) have to strive mightily to define it.

If the two quotes from these great sources of business wisdom make you feel like you wandered into a business school class where they forgot to give you the book, don't worry. Strategies are nothing more than your guides to creating the specific plans to shape your business for success. Following are some detailed examples.

Let's look at the computer networking business. (They're the companies who send a person to your office to make sure your computer connects to the main server; that you have virus protection and security; and all your crucial files are backed up.) There are four strategies in this business:

1. Show up when you say you will
2. Fix the problems the first time—no rework
3. Explain everything to the client in plain English
4. No surprises

That's it. A computer company that can deliver on these four strategies will be as busy as it wants to be, and will be able to charge a premium price.

Strategies can be deceptively simple. Simple, however, does not necessarily mean easy! Let's take the computer company strategy of "Show up when you say you will" from the example above. This should be relatively easy to do, right? Not exactly.

Think for a moment about all the factors that could interfere. Let's start with the human issues everyone faces: sore throats, flat tires, cars that won't start, sick kids. Then move to technical issues: the problem you came to fix at your first client's office is much more complex than you originally thought. That customer also forgot to mention to your dispatch person the 15 other things they need fixed. You accidentally brought the wrong part. You just made a mistake, and it will take an additional hour to fix.

You can see how "Show up when you say you will" can be extremely difficult to implement consistently, day after day. You can also see how this simple strategy could give birth to many goals and plans that would keep the company busy for years.

Taking the #1 strategy above "Show up when you say you will," let's see how it could be used to drive your activities year after year.

Strategy	Goal/plans, year one
Show up when you say you will	Create a centralized dispatch system
	Buy an engineering management software package by end of 1st quarter
	Train engineers by end of 2nd quarter
	Hire a dispatcher by the end of 3rd quarter
	Announce system to clients and go live by the end of 4th quarter

Strategy	Goal/plans, year two
Show up when you say you will	Create a training program for new engineers and dispatch personnel
	Train on how to decide whether to stay at current client, or leave to be on time for new client
	Cross-train engineers so they can back each other up
	Train dispatcher on what to do to handle engineers who are caught at a client with a severe technical issue

As you can see, implementing the plans dictated by this single strategy could guide the activities of the computer company for many years.

Now let's take a look at one of the fundamental strategies at Tesla, the electric car manufacturer. This isn't the only set of strategies for the car itself, but it's a key one: rather than viewing the car as a piece of machinery that cannot be substantially changed once it's manufactured, Tesla makes computers masquerading as cars. Therefore:

1. The car has an operating system like a computer, and like a computer is always connected to the Internet. Each time Tesla

adds a new feature it simply downloads an update to the car's operating system. Thus, the functionality of the car can be improved without having to swap out hardware.

2. To be able to treat the car as a computer it must have fewer moving parts. This led the company to the idea of making an electric car instead of using an internal combustion engine for power.

3. The car should be able to be purchased like a computer. So to buy one, you log into the Tesla website, select the model, features and color you want, then click to buy. The buyer has a certain amount of time to drive the car and can return it during that time for a full refund if she doesn't like it. This experience resembles the ease of buying a laptop rather than the customary ordeal of buying a car.

This isn't a definitive list of Tesla's strategies; it's a big company with lots of projects in the works. But these three simple strategies have spawned a multi-billion-dollar car company that has almost single-handedly moved the rest of the car business away from internal combustion engines to electric. This is the sign of an effective strategy: an easy-to-explain idea that when implemented, changes the world.

An example of another Fortune 500 company strategy is "health insurance for part- and full-time employees," as implemented by Starbucks.

This strategy, which stems from the founder's childhood experience of his family not having health insurance, helps Starbucks recruit and retain a more dedicated workforce than is normally seen in a retail environment. Recruiting and retaining a dedicated workforce is a very happy (and profitable) consequence of this strategy.

Here are some examples of strategies from a physical therapy practice:

1. Visibility in the appropriate communities.

2. Appropriate appearance, dress, and physical conditioning.

3. Scholarships availability for people in financial hardship to get physical therapy treatment.

4. Clear communication in everything we do.

Here are the strategies used by a financial consulting firm:

1. Everyone who's connected to us is committed to constant learning and improvement

2. Everyone who works with us takes 100% responsibility for their own results

3. Everything we do creates abundance for everyone involved

4. We work on a referral basis

The strategies you identify for your business will be simple also. You don't need a long list. Three to five strategies are enough to create a dynamic, profitable business.

Here are some strategy suggestions:

Health insurance for everyone

Strict confidentiality

Teamwork

Always the best person for the job

Creativity

Leading edge solutions

Everyone is certified

All our work is custom designed

All our work follows three set standards

Always deliver extra value

Do everything in-house—no outsourcing of any work

Support local economies

Sustainability

Convenience

Any color as long as it's black

We speak the language of the country you come from

We knock off designer goods at 25% of their price

Measurable results for clients

Solve business problems with technology

Do things right the first time

High-quality solutions

Continuous education for employees

Saving time

Low-cost solutions

Let the customer do some of the assembly to lower costs

Community involvement

Everything we do is green

Outsource everything but our core competencies

Diversity

Education of clients

On time, every time

Always the best parts

Always the most cost-effective parts

Build to last

Built to last one season

The tough part isn't identifying the strategies; it's implementing them.

If you are working in a group, select another partner (preferably someone you haven't worked with yet), and interview each other, answering questions 1–4 below. Copy your partner's answers into the sheets below, and have him/her do the same for you.

If you are working with a partner, interview each other, answering questions 1–4 below. Copy your partner's answers into the sheets below, and have him/her do the same for you.

If you are working alone, answer questions 1–4 below.

1. How do your clients wish you would work with them? (If you don't know, go ask them.)

    If you're doing everything they want already, that's great. List the things you're doing that make them so happy.

    Some examples might be:

    *   They want to find me on the Internet

    *   They want me to educate them

    *   They want me to be open 24 x 7 or 8–5, or only during evenings and weekends

    *   They want me to be referred by a trusted advisor

    *   They want me to cooperate with their lawyer

    *   They want me to be trustworthy

    *   They want me to be located on every corner

    *   They want me to do the same things every time I visit them

    *   They want me to create a new solution every time I visit.

2. What are industry leaders in your niche doing to win their awards? What strategies are they using to please their clients?

   Note: industry leaders can be defined in many ways. They might be the people who get recognized at your association's annual banquet for their innovations; they may be the people who get their pictures in the paper or in an industry trade magazine because of a change they've implemented in their company. They might be the biggest company in your industry, or the most inventive, or the most controversial. They also might be the people you feel jealous of when you open your monthly trade magazine and see them profiled on page one.

3. What are some things you know you need to do that you aren't doing now?

   Are any of these strategies? If so, list them:

4. Go back and look at the vision you wrote for your business in Module Two. Do any of the things you want to implement or change fall into the category of Strategies? If so, list them here:

5. Based on your answers above, list your strategies here:

Once you are satisfied with your strategies, transfer them to the *Passion, Plan, Profit* Business Plan Template on page 215.

Unique Selling Proposition

WHAT MAKES YOU DIFFERENT
FROM EVERYONE ELSE?

Insist on yourself; never imitate.

RALPH WALDO EMERSON

Lurking in every product which deserves success is a reason
for being and a reason for buying which is deeply felt by the
manufacturer and which, if captured and communicated, is
the best of all possible advertising, because it is honest and believable.

LEO BURNETT

There are four reasons why you must clearly understand and communicate your Unique Selling Proposition to your prospects (and
continue to reinforce it with your existing clients).

First, broad statements like these that you see every day: "We're the
cheapest." "We're the best." "We're committed to high quality." come
across at best as meaningless, and at worst, as lies.

Savvy customers (that's everyone) know that it's unlikely that your
business provides the cheapest products and services. There is only
one company that can be the cheapest. Chances are that company is
huge, with great economies of scale. That's not your small business,
nor would you want it to be. Competing on price alone is a tough way
to run a business and still create the profitability you need. If low
price is your only attraction, you'll find yourself cutting corners and
delivering subpar service. That's no way to honor your purpose.

Additionally, messages that say "we're the best," or "we're committed to high quality" are so general that your customers disregard them
altogether.

You do want to be the best at something specific, however, which is what this section of the workbook is designed to help you discover and articulate.

Second, if you don't tell your customers what makes your business different (and of course, better) than all the others, in very specific terms, your customers will define you themselves. They'll define you by the experiences they have; by how you make them feel when they work with you. These definitions will be much more nuanced than "best" or "high quality." You also may not like the ways your customers leap into the breach to define your business for you, if you aren't consciously defining yourself, and then actually acting that way.

Third, if your business isn't perceived as different than all the others in its market, every sale is a new conquest. When your marketing doesn't help prospective customers decide whether you might be right for them or not, you or your staff has to personally locate, and then personally convince, every new prospect.

The fourth and final reason to be clear on what makes your business unique is that your uniqueness sets you apart from the competition. All businesses have strong competition, and the more you create a real, tangible difference in your business, with products and services, a difference that your customers really care about, the more profitable and abundant your business will be.

This compelling marketing message, a short, pithy description of what you do, is called a "Unique Selling Proposition."

Your USP is the key to communicating what's great, and what's different, about your business.

Here are some memorable Unique Selling Propositions:

- All the news that's fit to print — *New York Times*, 1896
- The Antidote for Civilization — Club Med Vacation Resorts, 1982
- The Best Seat in the Concert Hall — Harmon Kardon (AM/FM
- Radio), 1956
- Betcha can't eat just one — Lays Potato Chips
- The Breakfast of Champions —Wheaties Cereal, 1935
- The daily diary of the American dream —*Wall Street Journal*-Newspaper

> The more you create a real, tangible difference in your business, with products and services, a difference that your customers really care about, the more profitable and abundant your business will be.

- The document company — Xerox
- Does she or doesn't she? — Clairol Hair Coloring, 1957
- Don't Leave Home Without It — American Express Card
- Everything you always wanted in a beer . . . and less — Miller Lite Beer
- The few, the proud, The Marines — US Marine Corps
- Finger Lickin' Good — Kentucky Fried Chicken, 1952
- Fly The Friendly Skies — United Air Lines, 1966
- Gets the red out — Visine eye drops
- Gets you so clean your mother won't know you — Mr. Bubble Bath Soap
- Good To The Last Drop — Maxwell House Coffee, 1959
- The Greatest Show on Earth — Barnum & Bailey Circus
- Have it your way — Burger King Restaurants
- Inexpensive, and built to stay that way— Subaru Automobiles
- The instrument of the immortals — Steinway & Sons Pianos, 1919
- Is it live, or is it Memorex?— Memorex Recording Tapes
- It helps the hurt stop hurting — Bactine Antiseptic
- It keeps going, and going, and going — Eveready Batteries, 1989
- It's not just a job. It's an adventure — United States Navy
- It takes a licking and keeps on ticking — Timex Watches
- The King of Beers — Anheuser-Busch
- Leave the driving to us — Greyhound Bus Company, 1957
- Like a Rock — Chevrolet Trucks, 1986
- Melts in your mouth, not in your hand — M&M Candies, 1954
- Nothing runs like a Deere — John Deere Tractors
- Put a tiger in your tank — Esso Gasoline, 1964
- Safety First. Always —Volvo
- Strong enough for a man, but made for a woman — Secret Anti-perspirant
- Tastes great, less filling — Miller Light Beer
- The Ultimate Driving Machine — BMW, 1975
- When it absolutely, positively has to be there overnight — Fed Ex, 1982

- When it rains, it pours — Morton Salt, 1911
- When you care enough to send the very best — Hallmark Cards, 1934
- The World's most popular music jukebox and online music and video store — Apple iTunes
- You get fresh, hot pizza delivered to your door in 30 minutes or less—or it's free — Domino's Pizza
- You get rid of dandruff — Head and Shoulders shampoo
- You get younger-looking skin — Oil of Olay

You might be able to glean your USP from one of your strategies. For example, Wal-Mart's leading strategy (low price) is also their USP.

Volvo's USP (Safety First) is also their leading strategy. BMW's USP "The Ultimate Driving Machine" is also their lead strategy. The FedEx USP "When it absolutely, positively has to be there overnight," is their primary strategy.

The USP for the computer business whose strategies are listed in Module Six might be "Proven Solutions to Solve Business Problems."

Or, "We Do Things Right the First Time."

As you can see, this is an inexact science. The most important part of this work is the *thinking* about what makes your business unique.

Your USP can evolve as your business changes.

This uniqueness will permeate all your marketing activities, from your website to your brochures, catalogs, voicemail message, signature line on your e-mails, and anywhere else where you tell prospective clients about how good you are. If the USP is short enough, you will also put it on your business cards.

If you're doing a good job in your business, you already have a unique selling proposition.

Ask your clients what it is. If you don't have clients yet, go back to your purpose. It will tell you.

If you are working in a group, select another partner (preferably someone you haven't worked with yet). Again, take notes for each other by trading workbooks and writing your partner's ideas in his or her book. Answer questions 1–5 below.

If you are working with a partner, trade workbooks, write your partner's answers to the question below in his book, and have him/her do the same for you. Answer questions 1–5 below.

If you are working alone, answer questions 1–5 below. Because you are working alone, it's especially important for you to talk to your clients about what makes you unique, if you haven't already. They are **the** ultimate source for this information.

1. Go back and look at the reasons you went into business (Module One). Is there anything about your purpose that makes you different from other businesses in your same niche? If so, write it here:

2. Go back and look at your values (Module Four). Are your values different than other businesses in your industry? Is there anything about your values that makes you unique? If so, write it here:

3. Go back and look at your strategies (Module Six). Are you doing things differently in your business that make you unique? If so, write these things here:

4. What do your clients/customers say about why they do business with you? What's unique about your business that makes them choose you over someone else who does the "same" work? (If you don't know the answer to this, go ask your clients. They'll tell you.) Write what your clients say that is unique about you, here:

5. Taking the information from questions 1–4 above, write a short sentence about what makes you unique. The space is purposely limited for each attempt. If you can, try to confine your USP to 8 words or less. If it is too difficult to condense it into a sentence, list the 2–5 things that make you different, as bullet points.

Attempt #1 _____

_____

Attempt #2 _____

_____

Attempt #3 _____

_____

Once you are satisfied with your Unique Selling Proposition, transfer it to the *Passion, Plan, Profit* Business Plan Template on page 215.

Strengths, Weaknesses, Opportunities, Threats

YOUR ANALYSIS FROM THE INSIDE OUT

He only profits from praise who values criticism.

HEINRICH HEINE

A key part of every business and every business plan is taking inventory. This doesn't mean simply counting the products you have on the shelf (if you even have products). It means taking inventory in the broadest sense. It means answering the question: "What's going on in my business" (the "internal" inventory), and "what's going on in my market," (the "external" inventory).

The traditional way to do this is to look at the Strengths and Weaknesses of the business, the Opportunities the business has, and the Threats it faces ("SWOT" for short.)

Strengths and weaknesses are internal to the company and are things you can control; opportunities and threats are external factors that you can only plan for and try to respond to when they occur.

An obsolete computer system is a weakness (you have control, in that you can purchase new computers).

An impending recession is a threat (at best you can only try to plan your response if one happens; you can't control whether it happens or not).

One place to start a SWOT inventory is to examine the competition.

- What are your competitors doing right and wrong?

- What are your competitors doing that you should be doing?

- What are they doing that you should not do?

Another place to gather information is to think about what your customers say.

- Do you have enough people to accomplish your mission?
- Too many?
- How is the quality of your product or service?
- Do customers want you to carry new or different products and services?

A third place to look is at your marketplace.

- How has it changed since you first went into business?
- How do these changes affect the way you serve your clients?
- Have new opportunities arisen?
- Do you have new competitors?

Let's look at an example. Take a specialty retail store in a tourist area that sells crafts from local artists. They lease a space on the main street, but the store is too small. The economy is great, but the traffic is seasonal because it gets cold in the winter and the tourists all go home.

They use a cool antique cash register, which prompts many comments from customers, along with the occasional offer to buy it.

Strengths (things the business can control):

1. Location in a tourist area where people are likely to buy crafts to take home
2. Connection to local artists: lower or no shipping costs, local artists may be more in touch with the aesthetics of the area and the kinds of crafts clients want
3. Able to respond quickly to new trends, demands by clients

Weaknesses (things the business can control):

1. Size: less buying power than larger retailers
2. Space is too small
3. 3. No computerized inventory system

Opportunities (things the business cannot control):

1. Economy is strong; lots of demand for their crafts

2. Local crafts are in style right now

Threats (things the business cannot control):

1. Business is seasonal

2. The landlord wants to sell the building

Many times, threats can be opportunities, and strengths can be weaknesses. For example, a company may be the best, fastest, and most efficient manufacturer of vinyl records. This could be a strength. Unfortunately, there is a limited market for vinyl records, so this strength is also a weakness.

Another company may be facing a wholesale change in the marketplace; witness the upheaval in the music business that has gone from records to CDs to streaming to who knows what next. This has posed an existential threat to record companies but a flood of opportunity for individual artists who no longer need the intermediary of a record company to reach their fans.

Answer the questions on the following pages to get a picture of what's happening inside and outside your business.

If you are working in a group, select another partner (preferably someone you haven't worked with yet), and interview each other, answering questions 1–4 below. Copy your partner's answers into the sheet below, and have him/her do the same for you.

If you are working with a partner, interview each other, answering questions 1–4 below. Copy your partner's answers into the sheet below, and have him/her do the same for you.

If you are working alone, answer questions 1–4 below.

1. What are you doing really well in your business? What do your clients rave about? What are you proud of? What have you created that you think is great? List those things below. They are the strengths of your business. Remember, strengths are things you have control over; that you (and your partners, employees, advisors) created, that you can change.

List the strengths of the business here:

1.

2.

3.

4.

5.

2. What are you doing that's not so great? What do you need to do that you aren't doing? Are your customers complaining about anything? Are there some aspects of your business that you know you need to change? These are the weaknesses of your business. Remember that weaknesses are like strengths, in that they are under your control.

List the weaknesses of the business here:

1.

2.

3.

4.

5.

3. What's going on in the outside world? Are things changing in ways that help you? Are people suddenly more interested in what your business provides because the economy is better or worse, or your neighborhood has gone upscale, or people are finally becoming accustomed to buying what you sell over the Internet? These are opportunities for your business. Remember that opportunities are good things that happen for your business that are outside your control.

List the opportunities for the business:

1.

2.

3.

4.

5.

4. What's going on in the outside world that's not so good for your business? Is the economy bad or good? Are standards changing in your industry that threaten what you sell? Do you have a lot more competition than you used to? These are threats to your business, which, like opportunities, are out of your control.

List the threats to the business:

1.

2.

3.

4.

5.

Once your SWOT analysis is complete, and before moving ahead, transfer these bullet points to the *Passion, Plan, Profit* Business Plan Template on page 215.

The Numbers

HERE MAY BE DRAGONS

The next three modules are about the numbers: forecasting your income, your expenses, and figuring out what your key measurements are. (Don't worry if you don't know what a key measurement is; I've explained it all in great detail in Module 11. You'll get it.)

Some of you reading this book are numbers-oriented. You like them. They behave for you. You are the envy of every heavily-right-brained person you have ever met. You will not have trouble with the next three sections. Go Forth and Forecast!

Some of you are not numbers-oriented.

You might be like my friend Deb, a nurse with thirty years' experience in health care. You would want to have her with you if you need someone to save your life, but she says things like: "I can't do math."

You might be a very right-brained person whose checkbook isn't balanced, who does his taxes by bringing the shoebox full of receipts to his accountant (and suffers the withering looks as a consequence), or who bailed out of basic math class freshman year of high school and never looked back.

It Doesn't Matter. You Can Do This Work.

What I am about to teach you is how to speak, "Number."

Number is a language all its own. It's the language your business speaks. It's the way your business tells you the whole truth about what's going on. People can make numbers lie, but in their natural state, numbers can't help themselves. They always tell the truth.

Your business is dying to talk to you. It's aching to tell you which customers buy the most, and which ones should be let go. It wants you to know how much money you made last year, and last month, and yesterday, and how that compares to the same time period the previous year. It wants to tell you which expenses are higher this month than they were last month, and it wants you to pay attention. It wants to tell you how profitable your biggest job was this month. It knows *everything* about what's going on. But to understand what it knows, you have to learn its language.

Imagine you were adopting a child from another country. If she were Russian, you'd need to pick up a few words of Russian, especially in the beginning, so you could understand each other. However, your Russian child will eventually learn to speak English. Your business never will. It will always speak Number. Your job is to learn how to understand what your business is telling you.

Anyone can learn to speak Number. The math skills required to speak Number are Addition and Subtraction, Multiplication and Division. That's it. Unless you dropped out of school in fourth grade (or even if you did), you already have all the math ability you need.

What makes Number look hard is not the math, it's the terminology. These next three modules will teach you all the jargon you need to know. Once you start working the step-by-step process of the first Number module, you'll see that you can do it.

You will need three kinds of help to finish the next three modules. I have done my best to provide you with the first kind, which is nothing more than encouragement.

The second kind of help is assistance in using a spreadsheet program. The one that comes on many computers is Microsoft Excel, but there are others you can use as well. It doesn't matter which one you pick. You just need to learn how to use it. The work in two of the next three modules, which is to create a business income and expense forecast covering the next twelve months, will be cumbersome and exhausting without one.

If you already know your way around a spreadsheet, that's great. If not, help is easy to find. If you have anyone in your family under the age of 25, any of them can lend a hand. Your local high school or community college can be a source of talented people with great computer skills. You can buy a book, or take a class either in person or online. Many of the software packages themselves have tutorials as part of the software. You don't need to become an expert. You just need to learn how to make the spreadsheet add, subtract, multiply, and divide.

The third kind of help is the "reasonableness test." You need someone to review your numbers to see if they make sense.

If you're working alone, get someone to agree to review your work when it's finished, and set the date with them now. Don't drag this out. If you are working with a partner and neither of you feels comfortable reviewing the other's work, do your work together, then get someone (CPA, coach, etc.) to review your work.

If you are working in a group, do your work in pairs. You can review your forecasting work in the group, member by member. If no one in the group feels comfortable performing the reasonableness test, hire someone to come in and review everyone's work.

Remember. You Can Do This. Don't be scared. And even if you are scared, do the work anyway. If you stayed awake during even a single semester of high school Spanish, you can learn to speak Number. It can also be helpful to take the worksheets and your laptop, if you have one, to a pretty place to do the work. Your local coffee bar can provide a festive setting. Turn the page, and let's get going.

WHAT TO DO IF YOU DON'T KNOW YOUR PRICES

Sometimes, people don't have a clear idea of what their products and services actually are, nor what prices they charge for their work. If you do know your prices, skip this section and dive straight into the income forecast in Module 9.

If this is you, don't despair. You are not alone. Many people, especially when they are first starting out, treat every job or product as custom, with a different price. Or they might simply be vague about their pricing. Or they might have a good sense of what each customer will pay, and charge a different price to each client just because they can.

Whatever the reason, if you don't have established prices for your products and services, it's now time to set them. It will help you gain even more clarity, give your business more financial stability and predictability, and get you off the hook about remembering all the different prices you've quoted to people.

You can use the worksheets below to establish prices for your products and services now. Once you fill in these tables, you will use these numbers to create the forecast using the directions starting on page 89.

The first worksheet below is for products. If you sell products, list each one in a separate box below, along with the price you are charging for the product. If you have a lot of products (more than ten), group them by price (low, medium, high), or by price range ($100–$200, $201–$500, $501–$1,000), or whatever makes sense to you.

Here are some examples to help you get started. Our first example is a computer networking firm that sells computers, software and installation services for fixed prices.

Their price list might start out like this:

Product name	Price
Small server (for networks up to 5 workstations)	$1,500
Medium server (for networks up to 20 workstations	$5,000
Large server (for networks up to 100 workstations)	$12,000
Small network installation	$1,000
Medium network installation	$5,000
Large network installation	$10,000
Network plan	$995
Security package (firewall, virus software installation)	$2,000

This business probably sells more products than are listed here, but this gives you an idea about what a product price list would look like.

The next example is a business that sells services by the hour. If you are a CPA, attorney, plumber, or other service business that bills by the hour, you can set your prices here. You may simply have one hourly rate for everything; if you do, skip to the next module and start forecasting.

But if you have different hourly rates for different types of services, you will need to set those prices. Here is an example of what a CPA firm's rates might look like:

Service type	Price
Audit services-small companies (less than 100 employees)	$195/hour
Audit services large companies (more than 101 employees)	$150/hour
Tax return preparation	$150/hour
Tax planning	$195/hour
Financial statement preparation	$125/hour
Partner review	$250/hour
Associate information gathering	$95/hour

It is possible that you sell both products and services. Let's look at a landscaping firm that sells both plants and the design and installation of landscaping for different hourly rates.

Product name	Price
Small bedding plants	$10 per flat
1 gallon plant	$12 each
5 gallon plant	$30 each
20 gallon plant	$95 each
Small landscape design (less than 500 sq. ft.)	$300
Medium landscape design (500–2,000 sq. ft.)	$995
Large landscape design (over 2,000 sq. ft.)	$175/hour
Planting labor	$50/hour
Project management	$75/hour

Now it's your turn. Use the form on the next page to list everything you sell, (or every group of things you sell), and the price for each one.

If you just sell products, or just bill by the hour, or some combination of both, it doesn't matter. You can use the grid below to list everything.

Once you've done this, you can proceed to the next module and do your income forecast.

PRICE LIST

Product or service name	Price

Good work! Now turn to the next page, and start forecasting.

The Numbers
YOUR INCOME

If you have built castles in the air, your work need not be lost;
that is where they should be. Now put the foundation under them.

HENRY DAVID THOREAU

In preparing for battle I have always found that plans are useless,
but planning is indispensable.

DWIGHT D. EISENHOWER

Part of the challenge in earning your principal income from your business is that any hiccups in your business revenue create painful repercussions in your personal life. In the next three sections you will create clarity by forecasting your income and expenses, and choose two or three key measurements to track your business results.

The first step in creating an income and spending plan for your business (a forecast), is to *estimate the income* your business will generate by product or service, month by month.

People always balk at this step. They say, "How am I supposed to forecast the future? I have no idea what will happen in the next 10 minutes, let alone next year." Or they say, "I'm not sure what my products or services are yet." Or, like my friend Deb, "I can't do math."

This is where you have to hitch up your pants and do this anyway. If you don't know what your products are exactly, or what their prices should be, do some research, then take a stab at it. This is the place to start stabbing.

Let's start with a word about products and services in general. First, if you have an existing business, you might be caught in the trap of treating every job as custom. "But," you argue, "I'm an architect (or a landscaper, or a computer network designer), and every job I do is custom."

Yes, that's true. However, the process you go through to design each house/building/yard/computer network should not be custom. You need to have a standardized process that you execute each time. You know how many hours it takes you (and your support people, if you have any), to design a small, medium, and large project. And you go through that process, take the same amount of time, and charge roughly the same amount, for each small, medium, or large job.

I realize that to make this estimate you will have to make some simplifying assumptions (like the square footage definition of a "small" or "medium" or "large" house in the case of the architect), and those assumptions won't be 100% accurate. But they'll be close. And making these assumptions, classifying (and thus clarifying) your work, will help immensely in understanding your business; which clients you want to pursue; and how many small, medium, and large projects you want to design this year to hit your revenue goal. You will forecast your jobs by size.

Another factor to consider is what happens if you can only create a certain number of "products" to sell each year. Take artists, for example. They're faced with a real dilemma. What if an artist can only produce 12 paintings or 10 ceramic pieces, or 15 fabric hangings, per year, and the sales from those pieces don't generate enough revenue? Not to mention having to nurture (or wrestle) their sometimes mercurial muse, who may not take well to being managed?

If you are an artist, look at your output as a product; categorize it into small, medium, and large pieces, and figure out how much time it takes to make each type of piece. Then you can understand how many pieces of each size you need to make and sell to hit your revenue goal.

Next, look around for other ways to earn money on your art besides selling the original work. Visual artists can make posters, cards, or other copies of their original images that can generate additional revenue.

You can teach others as part of your business. You can give keynote speeches, be an artist-in-residence at a school. There are many ways to earn money as an artistic person. Many excellent books have been written on this subject; check your favorite search engine for a list.

Let's pause for a moment to explode the myth of the starving artist. The last thing the world needs is to have our most creative people starving. If you are an artist, take it on yourself to treat your art like a business so that we can have more creative people supporting themselves with their art. Think about what a contribution to world peace that would be.

Now, back to our income forecast.

As I mentioned before, it is a *really good idea* to use a spreadsheet to do the math for you. If you can't operate a spreadsheet program, remember what I said about getting someone to help. This is prime saboteur-territory. Don't let not knowing stop you. You are simply doing your homework to learn to speak Number.

I have broken down this work into a series of questions. All you have to do is walk through the questions, step by step.

Here's the truth about forecasts. You could get yours totally right, or be 100% wrong, and it wouldn't matter. The benefit of doing the forecast is the clarity it brings you, not whether you predict next year's income to the penny.

Here's an example of someone who forecasted her income in a specific area correctly (actually, within $5.00), and what it did for her.

Leslie Keenan, the writer-muse who helped me finish the 1st edition of this book did her first income forecast years ago. She was a literary agent then, and was trying to forecast the royalties she would receive on a book that she had sold to a publishing house.

The only concrete information she had was the number of books that had been sold in the past six months. How in the heck was she supposed to estimate how many books would sell in the coming year?

She knew that book sales are strongest in the first six months of publication, so she took the sales figures she had and forecasted sales slowly falling off over the next year. She had no idea how much they would fall off, so she just guessed.

Then she calculated her standard commission on the mythical number of book sales she forecasted.

At the end of year she was within $5.00 of her forecast.

How did this help her? It showed her that she could prepare a sales forecast with limited (but important) information and still get pretty close to her actual sales number. This may be what happens to you.

Or, you might have this experience: A business coach (who will remain nameless), forecasted her income for the year, including revenue from two workshops per month. But she didn't do much of anything to make these workshops happen. She booked a room but did minimal publicity and marketing. She talked about writing the content for the second workshop but didn't finish it until the year was half over. So, neither the workshops, nor the revenue from them, materialized. She could have felt badly about this (and did, for awhile). Or she could have blamed herself or blamed the forecast for being so inaccurate.

Instead, she viewed the forecast as a teacher. It taught her that though she wanted to hold two workshops per month, in order to have them happen she had to do footwork: she had to market the workshops.

Falling short on the number of workshops she had forecasted was simply an indication that she hadn't tied enough (or any) marketing activities to her forecast to help the workshop, and the revenue, happen.

The other lesson that your forecast will teach you is: can your business support you? If, when you do your income forecast, and the business doesn't generate enough revenue to provide you with a comfortable living, *there is a problem*. Don't give up yet, though. Turn to page 158 for a list of suggestions to help you generate more revenue in your business.

You may still want to argue, especially if your business isn't up and running yet, about the impossibility of figuring out what to charge and how much you'll sell. Do it anyway. The Internet is a vast resource of other people's pricing, products, suppliers, and business models. You already know a lot about your business, even if you're just starting.

Take what you know (as Leslie did, in the example above) and make your best guess.

If you absolutely have no idea about what to charge, as a last resort, back into your prices by looking at the benefits your customers get from doing business with you. How much benefit do you provide? What is that benefit worth to your clients? Do you save them time? Help them do something they couldn't do without you? What is that worth?

I am not asking you to predict the future with total accuracy. I'm not even asking you to predict the future with any accuracy. I am asking you to take your best guess at what might happen, given reasonable effort on your part over the next twelve months.

After you pour your heart and soul into this forecast, I have some bad news. The second after you enter the last number, things will begin to change. Your clients will decide they love one product you didn't think would be a good seller, and shun another one you were sure they would adore. You will figure out how to deliver one of your key services twice as efficiently, which means you earn twice as much money as you thought you would on that service. Or you find out that to keep performing your most popular service, you have to invest in expensive new tools and education, making that service less profitable. There's no telling what will change, but change itself is certain.

That doesn't make the exercise useless. This forecast is necessary because it makes concrete the number of products you need to sell, or the number of hours you need to bill, or the number of clients you need to see, to earn the income you envision for yourself. Just because it's impossible to forecast this with accuracy doesn't mean it isn't crucial to do it anyway. Trust me on this.

Enough preparation. Let's start by looking at an example.

We are going to imagine that you sell an imported Italian fisherman's shirt. You sell it for $200 (it's a fancy shirt), and you think you will sell ten in the first month, increasing to 200 per month by the end of the year. Here's what your income forecast looks like:

Shirt merchant	Month					
	Jan	Feb	Mar	Apr	May	June
Shirt price	200	200	200	200	200	200
# sold	10	50	75	110	150	150
Total revenue	2,000	10,000	15,000	22,000	30,000	30,000

	July	Aug	Sept	Oct	Nov	Dec
Shirt price	200	200	200	200	200	200
# sold	160	160	170	180	190	200
Total revenue	32,000	32,000	34,000	36,000	38,000	40,000

Pretty straightforward. You multiply the price of the shirts by the number of shirts sold, which calculates your total revenue, month by month.

Let's take another example, using a CPA firm that bills by the hour.

They know how many hours they bill per month, and they know what they charge per hour. Their income forecast looks very similar to our shirt seller above, except that they are selling time, instead of a product.

The other difference in this income forecast is that the number of hours billed varies, up and down, throughout the year, instead of ramping up in a straight line like our shirt merchant. This business is cyclical:

I assumed Month One in the forecast below was January, which is the beginning of tax season for US accountants. Their workload ramps up through April, then they collapse in exhaustion for two months, then the workload bounces around, depending on whether it's the end of a quarter or year-end. Your business may be seasonal like this one. If so, reflect that seasonality in your forecast.

CPA firm	Jan	Feb	Mar	Apr	May	June
Hourly rate	150	150	150	150	150	150
# of hours billed	100	200	250	280	90	140
Total revenue	15,000	30,000	37,500	42,000	13,500	21,000

	July	Aug	Sept	Oct	Nov	Dec
Hourly rate	150	150	150	150	150	150
# of hours billed	130	130	150	150	200	200
Total revenue	19,500	19,500	22,500	22,500	30,000	30,000

Our last example will be a landscaping business. Because they combine both products (plants) and services (the landscaping itself), and because it would drive them crazy to forecast the number of trees, flowers, ground cover, and all the other plants one by one, they will forecast their income by size of client.

We will make some assumptions to simplify this forecast. First we will assume that there are three sizes of jobs (small, medium, and large).

Second, small jobs are $1,000, medium jobs are $5,000, and large jobs are $10,000. We are also going to assume that every job has the same ratio of plants to labor (i.e., a $1,000 job is made up of $600 of labor and $400 of plants; a medium job has $3,500 of labor and $1,500 of plants, etc.) I realize that this is a lot of simplification. If you have a situation like this, where your jobs contain both parts and labor, you'll have to remain vigilant that the assumptions you made are reasonably close to reality.

You can use this method to forecast your income if your jobs include a plethora of smaller components (such as a contractor for whom it would not be meaningful to forecast every nail he sells/uses in a job), or an architect, plumber, or even an interior decorator who also sells furniture/tile/window coverings, etc.

The small job forecast is listed below. Our landscaper would do this chart again, forecasting his medium and large jobs the same way.

Notice, this business is also seasonal.

Land-scaper	Jan	Feb	Mar	Apr	May	June
Small job price	1,000	1,000	1,000	1,000	1,000	1,000
# of jobs per month	5	6	15	15	15	20
Total revenue	5,000	6,000	15,000	15,000	15,000	20,000

	July	Aug	Sept	Oct	Nov	Dec
Small job price	1,000	1,000	1,000	1,000	1,000	1,000
# of jobs per month	25	27	15	5	5	3
Total revenue	25,000	27,000	15,000	5,000	5,000	3,000

Okay. Enough examples. Let's begin your income forecast.

Once you know how much of each product or service you need to sell (the part you can't control), you can figure out the footwork (i.e. marketing, the part you can control), to help those sales happen.

You have two choices. You can fill in the worksheet below to complete your forecast, or you can download a spreadsheet template at www.christystrauch.com/books. The template contains formulas that will do a lot of the calculating for you.

If you are working in a group, follow the directions below and estimate your income on your own. Then select another partner (preferably someone you haven't worked with yet), and review your work with him/her.

Have your partner look for obvious issues with your forecast, such as: are your prices too high (or, more likely), too low?

Are you forecasting selling 1,000 items a month when right now you're selling 25? Ask them to test for reasonableness. Adjust your forecast as necessary.

If you are working with a partner, follow the directions below and estimate your income based on these directions. Then review your work with your partner as described above.

If you are working alone, follow the directions below and estimate your income based on these directions. I strongly encourage you to review this forecast with your bookkeeper, your CPA, or another trusted advisor so they can help you test for reasonableness.

DIRECTIONS FOR ESTIMATING YOUR INCOME: PRODUCTS AND SERVICES

Note: if you create revenue by billing by the hour, skip to page 112 for directions and a template that you can use.

1. The months are numbered across the top one through twelve. Month 1 doesn't have to be January if you don't want it to be. If today is April 12, and you want the forecast to start in July, then Month 1 is July. Pick what month you want this forecast to start in, write it in the tiny space next to the number, then write the rest of the months across in order.

2. What is your most popular product or service? This will be Product #1 on the spreadsheet.

   Write the name of this product or service on the blank line in the first cell of the worksheet. ("Cell" is the term for each little box in a spreadsheet.)

3. How much do you charge for your most popular product or service? For example, if you are a car dealer, what is the average amount of money charged for each car? If you sell books, what is the average sale price of each book? If you install computer networks, you bill by the project, and your small network installations are the most popular, how much do you charge for a small network? If you are a landscaper, you also charge by the project, and your large landscaping jobs are the most popular, what do you charge for a large landscaping job?

   Enter this number in the first column to the right of "Product or Service #1"

4. How many of these products or services do you think you'll sell in a month?

   Fill in that number in the "Number of sales/month" cell right below the first cell.

5. Now multiply the average amount per sale, times number of sales per month.

   Put that number in the third cell down. This number is the total amount of revenue you will recognize in the month for this particular product or service.

6. Continue down the page and do this for every product or service you sell, for every month in the year.

7. Now add up the amounts in all the columns marked "Product # ___ total revenue/month" (they are in bold) and enter the number in the bottom row on pages 110–111. This is your total sales number, month by month.

8. If you are working in a group, pick someone and review your forecast with them. If you're working in a pair, review your forecast with each other. If you're working alone, finish the expense module below (Module 10), then take the whole thing to your bookkeeper or CPA.

Congratulations! You just did your first income forecast!! Don't stop here. You're not really finished until you figure out whether the income you forecasted will cover your expenses. You'll calculate that in the next module. Go to page 127 to begin your expense forecast.

INCOME CALCULATOR: PRODUCTS OR SERVICES

	Month				
	1	2	3	4	5
Product or Service #1 (write name on this line) _____ Enter the average dollar amount per sale in the boxes to the right:					
Enter the **Number of Sales** of this product or service per month in the boxes to the right:					
Product or Service #1 Total Revenue per Month (Multiply the average dollar amount by the number of sales and enter the result here.)					

Month						
6	7	8	9	10	11	12

INCOME CALCULATOR: PRODUCTS OR SERVICES, continued

	Month				
	1	2	3	4	5
Product or Service #2 (write name on this line) _____ Enter the average dollar amount per sale in the boxes to the right:					
Enter the **Number of Sales** of this product or service per month in the boxes to the right:					
Product or Service #2 Total Revenue per Month (Multiply the average dollar amount by the number of sales and enter the result here.)					

Month						
6	7	8	9	10	11	12

INCOME CALCULATOR: PRODUCTS OR SERVICES, continued

	Month				
	1	2	3	4	5
Product or Service #3 (write name on this line) _____ Enter the average dollar amount per sale in the boxes to the right:					
Enter the **Number of Sales** of this product or service per month in the boxes to the right:					
Product or Service #3 Total Revenue per Month (Multiply the average dollar amount by the number of sales and enter the result here.)					

Month						
6	7	8	9	10	11	12

INCOME CALCULATOR: PRODUCTS OR SERVICES, continued

	Month				
	1	2	3	4	5
Product or Service #4 (write name on this line) _____ Enter the average dollar amount per sale in the boxes to the right:					
Enter the **Number of Sales** of this product or service per month in the boxes to the right:					
Product or Service #4 Total Revenue per Month (Multiply the average dollar amount by the number of sales and enter the result here.)					

Month						
6	7	8	9	10	11	12

INCOME CALCULATOR: PRODUCTS OR SERVICES, continued

	Month				
	1	2	3	4	5
Product or Service #5 (write name on this line) _____ Enter the average dollar amount per sale in the boxes to the right:					
Enter the **Number of Sales** of this product or service per month in the boxes to the right:					
Product or Service #5 Total Revenue per Month (Multiply the average dollar amount by the number of sales and enter the result here.)					

Month						
6	7	8	9	10	11	12

INCOME CALCULATOR: PRODUCTS OR SERVICES, continued

	Month				
	1	2	3	4	5
Product or Service #6 (write name on this line) _____ Enter the average dollar amount per sale in the boxes to the right:					
Enter the **Number of Sales** of this product or service per month in the boxes to the right:					
Product or Service #6 Total Revenue per Month (Multiply the average dollar amount by the number of sales and enter the result here.)					
Total Sales (add up the numbers in the rows that are in bold above to calculate total sales by month)					

Month						
6	7	8	9	10	11	12

DIRECTIONS FOR ESTIMATING YOUR INCOME: BILLING BY THE HOUR

You have two choices. You can fill in the worksheet below to complete your forecast, or you can download a spreadsheet template at www.christystrauch.com/books. The template contains formulas that will do a lot of the calculating for you.

1. The months are numbered across the top of the chart, one through twelve. Month 1 doesn't have to be January if you don't want it to be. If today is April 12, and you want the forecast to start in July, then Month 1 is July. Pick what month you want this forecast to start in, write it in the tiny space next to the number, then write the rest of the months across in order.

2. What is your most popular service? This will be Service #1 on the spreadsheet. Write the name of this service on the blank line in the first cell of the worksheet. ("Cell" is the term for each little box in a spreadsheet.)

3. What is the hourly rate you charge for this service? Enter this first hourly rate in the first column, to the right of the cell that contains the name of the service.

   Here are some examples. If you are a CPA, you may charge different hourly rates for different types of work. Tax returns may be a certain hourly rate; audits another rate; financial statements, yet a third rate. You would forecast each of these types of services on separate lines in the spreadsheet below.

   OR, you may have different hourly rates for different levels of experience: partners in the firm charge the highest rate; managers less; and new hires the least. You would forecast the hours billed by partners on the first line, the hours billed by the managers next, and so on.

   You can create this forecast either way.

4. How many hours do you think you'll bill for this service in a month? Fill in those numbers in the "Number of Hours/ Month" row.

5. Now multiply the hourly rate for this service times the number of hours per month you plan to bill. Enter that number in the third row. This number is the total amount of revenue you will earn in the month, for this particular service at this hourly rate.

6. Continue down the page and do this for every service you sell that is a different hourly rate, for every month in the year.

7. Now add up the amounts in all the columns marked "Service #___ Total Revenue per Month" (they are in bold) and enter the number in the bottom row on pages 124–125. This is your total sales number, month by month.

8. If you are working in a group, pick someone and review your forecast with them. If you're working in a pair, review your forecast with each other. If you're working alone, finish the expense module below and take the whole thing to your bookkeeper or CPA.

Congratulations! You just did your first income forecast!

Don't stop here. You're not really finished until you figure out whether the income you forecasted will cover your expenses. You'll calculate that in the next module. Go to page 127 to begin your expense forecast.

INCOME CALCULATOR: SERVICES BILLED BY THE HOUR

	Month				
	1	2	3	4	5
Service #1 (write name on this line) _____ Enter the hourly rate for this service in the boxes to the right:					
Enter the Number of Hours of this service you want to bill per month in the boxes to the right:					
Service #1 Total Revenue per Month: multiply the hourly rate times the total number of hours and enter the result here:					

Month						
6	7	8	9	10	11	12

INCOME CALCULATOR: SERVICES BILLED BY THE HOUR, continued

	Month				
	1	2	3	4	5
Service #2 (write name on this line) ――――――――― Enter the hourly rate for this service in the boxes to the right:					
Enter the Number of Hours of this service you want to bill per month in the boxes to the right:					
Service #2 Total Revenue per Month: multiply the hourly rate times the total number of hours and enter the result here:					

Month						
6	7	8	9	10	11	12

INCOME CALCULATOR: SERVICES BILLED BY THE HOUR, continued

	Month				
	1	2	3	4	5
Service #3 (write name on this line) _____ Enter the hourly rate for this service in the boxes to the right:					
Enter the Number of Hours of this service you want to bill per month in the boxes to the right:					
Service #3 Total Revenue per Month: multiply the hourly rate times the total number of hours and enter the result here:					

Month						
6	7	8	9	10	11	12

INCOME CALCULATOR: SERVICES BILLED BY THE HOUR, continued

	Month				
	1	2	3	4	5
Service #4 (write name on this line) _____ Enter the hourly rate for this service in the boxes to the right:					
Enter the Number of Hours of this service you want to bill per month in the boxes to the right:					
Service #4 Total Revenue per Month: multiply the hourly rate times the total number of hours and enter the result here:					

Month						
6	7	8	9	10	11	12

INCOME CALCULATOR: SERVICES BILLED BY THE HOUR, continued

	Month				
	1	2	3	4	5
Service #5 (write name on this line) _____ Enter the hourly rate for this service in the boxes to the right:					
Enter the Number of Hours of this service you want to bill per month in the boxes to the right:					
Service #5 Total Revenue per Month: multiply the hourly rate times the total number of hours and enter the result here:					

Month						
6	7	8	9	10	11	12

INCOME CALCULATOR: SERVICES BILLED BY THE HOUR, continued

	Month				
	1	2	3	4	5
Service #6 (write name on this line) _____ Enter the hourly rate for this service in the boxes to the right:					
Enter the Number of Hours of this service you want to bill per month in the boxes to the right:					
Service #6 Total Revenue per Month: multiply the hourly rate times the total number of hours and enter the result here:					
Total Sales (add up the numbers in the rows that are in bold above to calculate total sales by month)					

Month						
6	7	8	9	10	11	12

The Numbers

YOUR EXPENSES

I am indeed rich, since my income is superior to my expense, and
my expense is equal to my wishes.

KAHLIL GIBRAN

The next step is to estimate your expenses, month by month.

In estimating your expenses for the next 12 months, it's helpful to know what you spent last year. If you don't have those records, I will give you some resources to help you estimate.

There are two kinds of business expenses: Cost of Goods Sold and Administrative Expenses (sometimes known as Overhead, or General and Administrative Expenses, or G & A Expenses). Let's begin by discussing the difference between them, and why accountants make us put these expenses in separate categories (and why we're grateful to them for making us do this).

The primary difference between Cost of Goods Sold (abbreviated, "COGS") and Administrative expenses is that COGS vary directly with the number of things you sell, while Administrative expenses stay the same no matter how much you sell.

Let's take a look at the total sales and COGS for one month, for a company that imports watches.

Our watch merchant sells watches for $100 each. He forecasted that he will sell 1,000 watches per month in January (Revenue of 1,000 watches x $100 each = $100,000), 1,200 of them in February, and 1,500 of them in March. So his sales (which he forecasted in the previous module) are:

Product	January	February	March
Watches	$100,000	$120,000	$150,000

(To simplify this, we're only going to look at the forecast for three months.)

The watches cost the merchant $30 each, so his COGS (cost of the watches) for month one is $30,000 (1,000 watches x $30 each = $30,000):

Total sales	January	February	March
Watches	$100,000	$120,000	$150,000
COGS			
Cost of watches	$30,000	$36,000	$45,000

As you can see, the total cost of the watches varies directly with the number of watches sold. If you sell 1,000 watches, you earn $100,000, and you have to pay out $30,000 for those 1,000 watches. If you sold zero watches, your cost of goods would be zero.

Let's keep going to see if there are more costs that change as you sell more watches (or as you sell fewer, but we don't want that).

If you're buying these watches from somewhere else, (say, importing them from France), you might need to pay freight. Because you pay more freight the more watches you sell, (or less, if you sell fewer), this also qualifies as COGS. To make things simple, we'll assume that you pay the freight each time you sell a watch.

Let's see what this looks like. We'll assume that the freight per watch is $5. So in January when we sold 1,000 watches, the freight would be $5,000 ($5 x 1,000 watches = $5,000). As the number of watches sold goes up, so does the freight cost.

Total sales	January (1,000 sold)	February (1,200 sold)	March (1,500 sold)
Watches	$100,000	$120,000	$150,000
COGS			
Cost of watches	$30,000	$36,000	$45,000
Freight	$5,000	$6,000	$7,500

You might have other expenses that vary directly with the number of items you sell, such as commissions to people who sell your goods for you. For instance, you might contract with a wholesaler who sells your watches to retail stores, and you pay that wholesaler $20 for each watch they sell for you. This would be entered under "commissions paid to others," under COGS. Here's what that looks like.

Total sales	January (1,000 sold)	February (1,200 sold)	March (1,500 sold)
Watches	$100,000	$120,000	$150,000
COGS			
Cost of watches	$30,000	$36,000	$45,000
Freight	$5,000	$6,000	$7,500
Commissions to others	$20,000	$24,000	$30,000

Once you have entered all your COGS, you can calculate an important number; your Gross Profit. This is the amount of profit you make on your product, before you factor in the other costs of running your business (like the phone bill, rent, etc.)

Here's what the spreadsheet looks like now:

Total sales by month	January (1,000 sold)	February (1,200 sold)	March (1,500 sold)
Watches	$100,000	$120,000	$150,000
COGS			
Cost of watches	$30,000	$36,000	$45,000
Freight	$5,000	$6,000	$7,500
Commissions to others	$20,000	$24,000	$30,000
Total COGS	$55,000	$66,000	$82,500
Total gross profit	$45,000	$54,000	$67,500

Again, total COGS varies directly with the number of watches sold (i.e. more watches sold, higher COGS).

Why would you want to look at your Cost of Goods Sold and Gross Profit separately from your other costs? Here are some reasons:

1. If these numbers are out of whack, you have to fix them before you commit to this business. If your Cost of Goods sold is too high, your business won't make a profit. You won't generate enough revenue by selling your product to cover the overhead, like the phone, rent, computers, and all the other things you need to run your business. It's good to find this out before you rent an office or hire anyone.

2. The Gross Profit numbers help you compare your business results to other businesses doing the same thing. Other businesses in your niche may have wildly varying costs for rent, utilities, employees, etc., but you will all have relatively similar costs for your products. Comparing your COGS to other similar businesses' COGS will show you where you either have a competitive advantage in the cost of your products, or where you might need to cut costs (or, increase your quality and raise prices. What the heck.) Every industry has target Gross Profit

percentages. You can get a book from the library or check out Internet sites to see if you are as profitable as other people in your industry.

3. You have the most leverage (i.e., where making changes can have the biggest impact) in two places: how much you sell, and how much your products/services cost. If you don't track these numbers separately, it's tough to know what's happening with them, which then makes it difficult to make changes.

Using the watch example above, let's first see what would happen if your COGS is out of whack.

Assume your watches cost $70 each instead of $30. Also assume that the rest of your expenses (things like rent, your salary, etc., which we will discuss in more detail in a moment) were $45,000 per month (plus, to cut costs, we stopped selling to wholesalers so we didn't have to pay commissions to others).

Original situation: cost of watches is $30 each.

Total sales	January	February	March
Watches	$100,000	$120,000	$150,000
COGS			
Cost of watches	$30,000	$36,000	$45,000
Freight	$5,000	$6,000	$7,500
Total COGS	$35,000	$42,000	$52,500
TOTAL gross profit	$65,000	$78,000	$97,500
General/admin expenses	$45,000	$45,000	$45,000
Net profit	$20,000	$33,000	$52,500

In the situation above, the COGS is at the price where you can make a profit at your current sales volume of 1,000 watches in January, 1,200 in February and 1,500 in March.

Now look what happens in the New, Bad Situation: Cost of watches is $70 each.

Total sales	January	February	March
Watches	$100,000	$120,000	$150,000
COGS			
Cost of watches	$70,000	$84,000	$105,000
Freight	$5,000	$6,000	$7,500
Total COGS	$75,000	$90,000	$112,500
TOTAL gross profit	$25,000	$30,000	$37,500
General/admin expenses	$45,000	$45,000	$45,000
Net profit	–$20,000	–$15,000	–$7,500

With the COGS this high, you have to sell a lot more watches to be profitable. This problem would need to be fixed before you started your business.

Okay. You have just mastered the concept of Cost Of Goods Sold. Many new accounting students have fallen by the wayside, fainting and exhausted, in the face of these concepts that you have just learned. Way to go!

Take a deep breath. We have one more expenses concept to go.

Now that you see what COGS is, let's look at the other kind of expenses: the ones that are fixed; that don't vary (or care) whether you sold 3 or 30,000 watches this month.

Remember, these expenses go by different names. Sometimes they're called Fixed Expenses. Sometimes they're called General and Administrative Expenses, and sometimes they're called Overhead. Their primary characteristic is that they don't change, no matter what you sell or don't sell this month.

I've made a list of many of the standard fixed expenses on the spreadsheet that you will be using to estimate your businesses' expenses. Almost everyone has to pay for a phone, an internet connection, office supplies, postage, a computer, etc. I also left space for other costs that may be unique to your industry.

I've mentioned this already, but I'm going to emphasize it one more time. The reason these expenses are called "fixed" is because they don't change, no matter how much you sell. Your landlord doesn't care how many shirts your customers bought this month. He just wants his rent. Because of this, it's important to watch your spending. Many a small or start-up business has folded under the weight of heavy fixed expenses.

Outsource everything you can. This means instead of hiring your own employees to do things for you, hire companies who do those services. That way you don't have people on your payroll before you can afford them.

Single individuals in business for themselves, and companies, provide part-time (or even full-time) services in many areas: assistants, bookkeepers, receptionists, secretaries, and even technical services like computer, civil, and many other kinds of engineers. You can be much more flexible in using more or less of their services as you need and as your cash flow dictates, than you could ever be with an employee's time. Employees will expect a regular paycheck regardless of your sales volume, which makes them a fixed expense as well.

You must conserve your cash. It's not an accident that people say cash is the lifeblood of a business. Without it, your business dies. And we don't want that.

You are about to see what your financial picture needs to look like for you to achieve your goals. This is one of the most important exercises you will ever do.

It's important to watch your spending. Many a small or start-up business has folded under the weight of heavy fixed expenses.

Outsource everything you can. This means instead of hiring your own employees to do things for you, hire companies who do those services. That way you don't have people on your payroll before you can afford them.

If you are working in a group, follow the directions below. Then select another partner (preferably someone you haven't worked with yet), and review your work.

Have your partner look for obvious issues with your expenses, such as: do you have enough allocated for various crucial expenses, like computers, accounting services, telephone? Did you put in your salary? Business savings account (which should ultimately total six months of your business expenses)? Taxes? Ask them to test for reasonableness. Make adjustments as necessary.

If you are working with a partner, follow the directions below and estimate your expenses based on these directions, then review your work with your partner.

Have your partner look for obvious issues with your forecast as described above. Ask them to test for reasonableness. Make adjustments as necessary.

If you are working alone, follow the directions below and estimate your expenses. I strongly encourage you to review this forecast with your bookkeeper, your CPA, or another trusted advisor so they can help you test for reasonableness.

You can download a spreadsheet template at www.christystrauch. com/books which contains formulas that will do a lot of the calculating for you.

DIRECTIONS FOR ESTIMATING YOUR EXPENSES (COGS and General and Administrative)

Note: If you sell multiple products with different Cost of Goods Sold for each, read the directions below, and use the form beginning on page 146.

If you don't have any COGS because you don't sell products, skip pages 138–139 and start entering your expenses beginning on page 140.

1. Using the spreadsheet that follows these directions, fill in your monthly sales estimate across the top, in the line marked "Total Sales" (Transfer the Total Sales numbers you entered on the last line of your Income Worksheet, which is the total sales, month by month, for all products and/or services, or work billed by the hour, from the worksheets on pages 110–111 or pages 124–125.

2. Fill in your expenses. This sheet contains many of the most common expenses incurred by businesses. You won't necessarily use all the blanks. If you don't make a product, for example, then you won't have any "Cost of Goods Sold."

   If you do sell products, each product might have a different cost. In fact, chances are excellent that they do. If that is the case, use the form beginning on page 146 that will give you space to list more than one Cost of Goods Sold.

3. It is helpful in estimating your General and Administrative expenses if you know what you spent last year. If you didn't have a business last year or you didn't keep track, get help. Some possible sources of help are your bookkeeper/CPA, the person or people you're doing this work with, your friends who have businesses, competitors outside your area (we love to help people, just not our competitors down the street), and of course, the Internet.

4. There are lines in this chart for Business Savings Account and Income Taxes. These are real categories for which you need cash. To start out, you can set aside 15–20% of your net profit for taxes, and 10% of the net profit for your business savings account.

5. Don't forget to put in your own salary. Business owners (to the great consternation of their families) act as if their salary is the number that is left over after everyone else is paid. Do not do this. Your bookkeeper/CPA will argue with you about putting it into your expenses, and they may want to treat your salary differently. This doesn't matter. Put your full, gross salary in as part of your expenses in this exercise. Why? Because you can see in black and white whether your business can support you. If you find out it can't, heed the advice in question #6.

6. Often people find that they underestimate their expenses. When all the expenses are filled in, it may become obvious that the business isn't generating enough revenue. This is very common. Go back to your income estimates and see if there is a way to increase them. Look at your expenses and see if there are places you can cut. If these measures aren't enough, turn to page 158 for more suggestions.

7. Once all the expenses are filled in, total them, subtract them from the income, and see what your bottom line is. The "bottom line" is the number that is at the bottom of your spreadsheet, resulting from subtracting all your expenses from your sales. We want this number to be positive.

   "Bottom line" is imprecise. People will argue what expenses should be included. Sometimes people leave out their own salary (but of course we won't do this here), or other expenses that might not be related to daily operations. In your case, you will include all your expenses, so you can get a clear picture of how much profit your business is making, taking everything into consideration.

   We are operating under the idea that "Cash is King," which is why I am asking you to list every expense. In addition to high fixed expenses, the other thing that kills companies (even profitable ones), is running out of cash. It is possible to be profitable and still go out of business if you run out of cash. Hard to believe, but true.

Note: Time can also be a Cost of Goods Sold. Even though you probably won't be able to enter this cost on your expense forecast, you should create a system to track it. This is especially true if you exchange time for money (such as attorneys, CPAs, plumbers, and other people who charge by the hour). The time you spend on a job is a concrete expenditure of your energy and resources, so you need to factor it in as if it were a monetary expense. This is even more crucial if you do fixed-price projects that include time. You must make sure that your fixed-price includes all your time, especially the preparation and project management time, two areas where people tend to underestimate.

If you do charge by the hour, you will have forecasted the number of hours you will bill in the Income Forecast section in Module Nine. As part of tracking your expenses, you need to track your actual time spent on billable activities. There are software packages that can do this for you, but don't wait to start tracking your time if you haven't yet found the perfect package. With some discipline you can track your time in a spreadsheet, or by hand.

INCOME STATEMENT WORKSHEET, INCLUDING COGS AND GENERAL/ADMIN EXPENSES

	Month				
	1	2	3	4	5
Total sales (from Income Calculator)					
COGS					
Commissions to others					
Discounts/returns					
Cost of product					
Freight					
Cost of labor					
Other _____					
Other _____					
Other _____					
Other _____					
Total cost of goods sold (COGS)					
Gross profit (Sales minus COGS)					

Month						
6	7	8	9	10	11	12

MONTHLY ADMINISTRATIVE EXPENSES

	Month				
	1	2	3	4	5
Accounting					
Auto					
Bank fees					
Books/magazines					
Computer expenses					
Dues					
Entertainment					
Gifts					
Health insurance					
Legal					
Licenses					
Marketing					
Office supplies					
Payroll taxes					
Postage					
Printing					
Professional services					

Monthly Administrative Expenses continues on page 142

Month						
6	7	8	9	10	11	12

MONTHLY ADMINISTRATIVE EXPENSES, continued

	Month				
	1	2	3	4	5
Rent					
Repairs					
Retirement					
Salaries-administration					
Salaries-technical					
Salary-owner					
Telephone					
Training					
Travel					
Utilities					
Other _____					
Other _____					
Other _____					
Other _____					
Total admin expenses					

Month						
6	7	8	9	10	11	12

MONTHLY INTEREST, TAXES, BUSINESS SAVINGS ACCOUNT EXPENSES

	Month				
	1	*2*	*3*	*4*	*5*
Interest expense					
Income taxes					
Business savings account					
Total interest, taxes, business savings					
Total all non-COGS expenses (Total admin expenses from pages 142–143 plus Total interest, taxes, savings from line above)					
Net income (Total gross profit from the bottom line on pages 138–139 minus Total all non-COGS expenses from the line above)					

Month						
6	7	8	9	10	11	12

INCOME STATEMENT WORKSHEET, INCLUDING COGS AND GENERAL/ADMIN EXPENSES

Use this form if you have multiple products, each with different costs

	Month				
	1	2	3	4	5
Total sales (from Income worksheet)					
COGS					
Product 1: _____					
Commissions to others					
Discounts/returns					
Cost of product					
Freight					
Cost of labor					
Product 2: _____					
Commissions to others					
Discounts/returns					
Cost of product					
Freight					
Cost of labor					

Income Statement Worksheet continues page 148

Month						
6	7	8	9	10	11	12

INCOME STATEMENT WORKSHEET, INCLUDING COGS AND GENERAL/ADMIN EXPENSES, continued

	Month				
	1	2	3	4	5
COGS					
Product 3: _____					
Commissions to others					
Discounts/returns					
Cost of product					
Freight					
Cost of labor					
Product 4: _____					
Commissions to others					
Discounts/returns					
Cost of product					
Freight					
Cost of labor					

Income Statement Worksheet continues on page 150

Month						
6	7	8	9	10	11	12

INCOME STATEMENT WORKSHEET, INCLUDING COGS AND GENERAL/ADMIN EXPENSES, continued

	Month				
	1	2	3	4	5
COGS					
Product 5: _____					
Commissions to others					
Discounts/returns					
Cost of product					
Freight					
Cost of labor					
Product 6: _____					
Commissions to others					
Discounts/returns					
Cost of product					
Freight					
Cost of labor					

Income Statement Worksheet continues on page 152

Month						
6	7	8	9	10	11	12

INCOME STATEMENT WORKSHEET, INCLUDING COGS AND GENERAL/ ADMIN EXPENSES, continued

	Month				
	1	2	3	4	5
Total cost of goods Sold (COGS) for all products					
Gross profit (Sales minus COGS)					
Monthly administrative expenses					
Accounting					
Auto					
Bank fees					
Books/magazines					
Computer expenses					
Dues					
Entertainment					
Gifts					
Health insurance					
Legal					

Income Statement Worksheet continues on page 154

Month						
6	7	8	9	10	11	12

INCOME STATEMENT WORKSHEET, INCLUDING COGS AND GENERAL/ADMIN EXPENSES, continued

	Month				
	1	2	3	4	5
Licenses					
Marketing					
Office supplies					
Payroll taxes					
Postage					
Printing					
Professional services					
Rent					
Repairs					
Retirement					
Salaries-administration					
Salaries-technical					
Salary-owner					
Telephone					
Training					

Income Statement Worksheet continues on page 156

Month						
6	7	8	9	10	11	12

INCOME STATEMENT WORKSHEET, INCLUDING COGS AND GENERAL/ADMIN EXPENSES, continued

	Month				
	1	2	3	4	5
Travel					
Utilities					
Other _____					
Other _____					
Total admin expenses*					
Interest expense					
Income taxes					
Business savings account					
Total interest, taxes, business savings					
Total all non-COGS expenses (Total admin expenses* from above plus Total interest, taxes, business savings from line above)					
Net income (Total gross profit from bottom line on pages 152–153 minus Total non-COGS expenses from the line above)					

Month						
6	7	8	9	10	11	12

WHAT YOU SHOULD DO IF YOUR INCOME DOESN'T ADEQUATELY COVER YOUR EXPENSES, INCLUDING YOUR SALARY

If you followed directions and even went back one or two times to revise your assumptions, and your income still doesn't cover your expenses including your salary, don't give up. Many people have that experience the first time they do a forecast.

As long as you are doing great work in your business, raising prices is the first place to look if your forecast shows a shortfall. Look hard at this. People who are used to charging less than the going rate for their goods and services, even though those goods and services are high quality and provide great value to their clients, automatically assume all their customers will desert them if they increase their prices. They won't even entertain it. If you haven't raised your prices in a year, or you're at the bottom or even the middle of the price scale in your industry, raise your prices!

Many times I see people attract more business, not less, when they increase prices. Unless you're trying to raise them by 50% in one fell swoop (and there is probably a scenario where even this could make sense), a price increase signals to your clients that you're serious about staying in business.

If raising prices truly is not an option, here are four other alternatives you can try to help your income cover your expenses.

1. Look at how you might add more clients/customers to something you're doing already. For example, if you make money teaching workshops, can you add five more people to each workshop you're already doing? You're already spending the money and time to do the workshop; five additional people might bring in the needed revenue without incurring much more than the cost of extra materials.

2. Is there a service (or additional products) that naturally occur from the product(s) you already sell? Do you sell something that people would love to pay you to install for them? Or

warranty for them? Or sell accessories to them to help use the product better? Or teach them how to use the product in the first place? Or pay you to deliver it? Look around and see if there are products or services you could add to the products you're already selling that would serve your clients even better (or better yet, if you already have clients, ask them what they would want more of).

A great example of this is a truck I saw parked outside a big electronics store. If you don't have your own truck, you can rent one from them to haul home the 52" flat-screen TV you just bought. Think how happy their clients are, that for an extra $25 or $50, they can bring the TV home right now and not worry about roping Uncle Dave or the neighbor next door into delivering it for them.

3. If you're in the service business, same question. Is there a product that would pair naturally with your services? Should you add a guided meditation series as a product you make available to your therapy clients? Could you sell beautiful notebooks and pens to the writers you coach? Look around, and again, if you do have clients, ask them.

4. Do you find yourself explaining the same things over and over to your clients or prospects? Could that be turned into a training class that you could sell?

5. Would it make sense for your clients to buy from you more frequently? Would your clients get greater benefit from your business if they used you more often? I worked with a martial arts dojo that didn't let people sign up month by month; their policy was that to get the full benefit from the training, you had to sign a contract that obligated you to come for a year. That policy was good for their cash flow, obviously, but they felt it was also better for the client. Their experience was that for people to really learn the skill, they had to practice it for a year.

People who sell products and people who sell services have a lot to teach each other. Ask yourself if your product would benefit from a service being added to it and sold as a package. Ask yourself if your service could benefit from a product being added to it and sold as a package. You might be surprised at the ideas you generate when you view your product as a service, or your service as a product.

Notice I didn't suggest "work harder" as one of the options to increase your income. Look around for ways to add to your product/ service line instead of turning yourself into a workaholic. Even though it's very rewarding, you may already realize that owning your own business isn't for sissies. We need our rest to be able to serve our clients (and friends and families) the way we want and need to.

Don't give up if your forecast doesn't show enough income the first time, or even the third or fourth time. Go back and answer the questions above and see if there is a way to change what you're doing so your business can serve its clients profitably.

Bonus Section #1
BREAK-EVEN CALCULATION

First I'll show you how to do this, then I'll explain why this information is very interesting, crucial, and downright cool to know.

First, the definition. Your break-even point is the exact amount of revenue you need to cover all your General/Administrative/Overhead expenses every month. Including your salary, of course. So it could be the exact number of shirts our shirt seller needs to sell each month.

Or it could be the number of hours you need to bill per month, if you work by the hour. Or it's the number of piano lessons you need to give, or the number of patients you need to see each month.

We'll look at our watch merchant to illustrate how this works.

To do this calculation, we need to know the gross profit our watch merchant makes on each watch. He sells each watch for $100. Each watch costs $30, and the freight per watch is $5, so the total COGS is $35.00. He makes $65.00 per watch. Here's the calculation:

Sale price of one watch	$100.00
COGS	
Cost of watch	$30.00
Freight	$5.00
Total COGS	**$35.00**
Total gross profit per watch	**$65.00**

Next, we need to know how much our watch merchant's General/Administrative Expenses are. In our illustration on page 131, we said he spent $45,000 per month. When you do this for yourself, use your real numbers.

To calculate the break-even point, we take the total monthly expenses of $45,000 and divide this number by $65 (the total cost of goods sold per watch). This tells us that our watch merchant needs to sell 692.3 watches to break even; that is, to cover all his costs and have no money left over.

Here is the math:

Watch revenue (if he sells 693 of them)	$69,300
COGS	
Cost of watches (693 x $30/watch)	$20,790
Freight (693 x $5/watch)	$3,465
Total COGS (cost of watches added to cost of freight)	$24,255
Total Gross Profit (Total sales minus Total COGS)	$45,045
Total admin expenses	$45,000
Total net profit	$45

Note: we only got $45 of net profit because of rounding error. In this example, we used 693 watches; when our seller sells 692.3 watches, he breaks even exactly. Except for our rounding error of $45, every cent he made from selling his watches was spent on business expenses.

Now let's look at the magic that happens when you sell more than your break-even point.

We'll use the same example, except this time, instead of our watch vendor selling 693 watches, he sells 800 of them. Look at the math:

Watch revenue (if he sells 800)	$80,000
COGS	
Cost of watches (800 x $30/watch)	$24,000
Freight (800 x $5/watch)	$4,000
Total COGS (cost of watches added to cost of freight)	$28,000
Total gross profit (Total sales minus Total COGS)	$52,000
Total admin expenses	$45,000
Total net profit	$7,000

So what's the magic? That the gross profit on every watch he sells, beyond the 692.3-watch break-even point, goes into his pocket (except for the part he has to pay in taxes). He can spend it on new computers, marketing, or some other business expense; save it, pay himself a larger salary, make a donation to his favorite charity, or any combination of the above. The possibilities are endless.

How does this work for someone who sells services? Here's an example.

We'll look at a doctor (although this example works for anyone who bills by the hour; CPAs, plumbers, chiropractors, massage therapists, etc.).

Our doctor doesn't have a Cost of Goods Sold; her costs (like rent, receptionist, utilities, etc.) are all administrative. They don't vary no matter how many patients she sees.

This is how her break-even point looks:

Total admin expenses	$45,000 per month
divided by the doctor's hourly rate	÷ $350 per hour
Equals the number of hours per month she must work to break even	129 hours

So our doctor must work 129 hours a month at $350 per hour just to break even. If she worked (and could bill) a full 40 hours a week, every hour billed between 129 and 176 (there are 176 working hours in an average month, at 40 hours/week) would generate revenue that she could use to invest in the business, to save for retirement, or whatever she wants. This is what that would look like:

Monthly revenue ($350/hour x 129 hours per month)	$45,150
COGS	0
Total gross profit (Total sales minus Total COGS)	$45,150
Total admin expenses	$45,000
Total net profit	$150

Working and billing 40 hours a week, she would generate another $16,600 per month beyond her break-even point. Of course, if she works that hard, she'll have to spend the additional revenue on vacations and spa treatments.

$350 per hour x 176 hours per month	$61,600
COGS	0
Total gross profit (Total sales minus Total COGS)	$61,600
Total admin expenses	$45,000
Total net profit	$16,600

I can hear some of you wondering: "What about me? I sell products AND services." Excellent question. Here's what that looks like. Let's take a computer business that sells computers AND installation services. We'll make the following assumptions:

1. Their Overhead/Administrative expenses are $45,000 per month, like the examples above

2. They sell $50,000 worth of computers every month

3. The cost of the computers is $40,000

4. They bill their services at $150 per hour

Look at what happens with the product side (the computer sales) of this business, assuming the numbers above:

Computer revenue per month	$50,000
COGS	
Cost of computers	$40,000
Total gross profit (Total sales minus Total COGS)	$10,000

The business makes $10,000 per month on computer sales, so $10,000 of their $45,000 of Administrative expenses is covered.

The next step is to figure out how many hours of installation time the business needs to bill, to make up the other $35,000 of expenses. That formula looks like this:

Total administrative expenses	$45,000
Amount covered by computer sales	–$10,000
Left to cover	$35,000

The Number of Hours needed to cover $35,000 is:

Remaining administrative expenses	$35,000
Divided by the hourly rate	÷$150
Equals the number of hours that need to be billed per month to break even	233

Let's look at the whole picture:

Computer revenue per month	$50,000
COGS	
Cost of computers	$40,000
Total gross profit (Total sales minus Total COGS)	$10,000
Service revenue (234 hours billed at $150 per hour)	$35,100
Total revenue (both from services billed AND computers sold)	$45,100
Administrative expenses	$45,000
Total net profit (Total Revenue minus Administrative Expenses)	$100

The profit on every computer they sell after selling $40,000 worth of them; AND the revenue from every hour they bill beyond 234 hours is profit.

To recap: Why is it absolutely crucial to know your break-even point?

1. So you know how many things you need to sell/services you need to provide to cover ALL your expenses.

2. So you can have a plan for the additional profit when you do exceed the break-even point with your sales. (Which is a likely outcome of your business, because you are so clear about what you're doing and how it benefits your clients).

Before I end this section I want to reiterate one point. Administrative expenses *include* your salary. Your wage is not the money that falls out the bottom of your income and expense statement after everyone else is paid. You *must* pay yourself an ample salary. Your business will not thrive if you aren't thriving along with it. If neither you nor the business is thriving, make sure you're marketing regularly, and look at page 158 for more ideas on how to increase sales. Here is a worksheet to calculate your break-even point. Use the worksheet below or the template at www.christystrauch.com/books to calculate your break-even point.

BREAK-EVEN CALCULATION QUESTIONS FOR PRODUCTS

Use this set of questions to calculate your break-even point if you sell products only. If you sell services, skip to the directions on page 171. If you sell both products and services, skip to the directions on page 172. If you only sell one product, you only need to answer questions 1, 3, 4 and 6 below. Count yourself lucky.

1. Go back and get your "total revenue for the year" number you forecasted in the Income section (Module Nine). This number is the *total* sales you forecasted for the next 12 months, so you will have to add up the income, month by month, for all your products that you forecasted on the last line of pages 110–111. Write that total sales number here:_____

2. Once you have the total sales number for the year that you calculated in #1, next you will figure out what percentage of your total sales each product makes up. Here's how to do this.

    A. Total the sales for your first product for the whole year (12 months). Get this number by adding up the total sales of your first product from the line called "Product or Service #1 Total Revenue per Month" from the worksheet on pages 100–101.Write that number here:_____

    B. Divide the number in "A" by the total revenue you are forecasting for the year (the number in "1" above.)

	Total revenue for product #1
Divided by	**÷Total revenue for all products for the year**
Equals	**The percentage of your total revenue this product**

    C. This will tell you what percentage of your Total Revenue this specific product will represent. Write that percentage here:_____

For example: You want your business to sell a total of $1,200,000 for the year (answer to question 1 above).

You want to sell $400,000 worth of your bestselling watch (answer to question 2A). To determine what percentage $400,000 is of $1,200,000, you will divide $400,000 by $1,200,000.

Amount of sales of your bestselling watch	**$400,000**
Divided by the total sales of all watches	**÷$1,200,000**
Equals	**.33**

This tells us that you want 33% of your total revenue to be made up of sales of your bestselling watch.

Repeat the work in question two above for *every* product you sell until you have gone through all your products. *Note:* If you have hundreds of them (or even tens), group them into logical categories (probably by price) to reduce the number of products you have to do this calculation for, or you will drive yourself crazy.

3. What are your Total Expenses per month? Write this number, from the "Total All non-COGS Expenses" line which you will find on either the expense worksheet on pages 144–145, or pages 156–157, here: _____ .

   Note: if you have created a sophisticated forecast that has different Administrative expenses by month because your expenses are seasonal, average them across the 12 months and use that number for this exercise.

   However, if your Administrative expenses are significantly higher in some months compared to others, you will need to pay very close attention to your cash flow. Use the directions in the bonus section that follows to help you make sure you don't run out of cash.

4. Figure out the gross profit of each product you sell. To do this, subtract the sale price of each thing you sell from the Cost of Goods Sold for this product, from the expense sheets on pages 138–139 or pages 146–151. If you are grouping your products, take the average sales price of the group and the average Cost of Goods Sold to do this

calculation. Don't forget to add in all the costs that go with the Cost of Goods Sold, like freight, commissions to others, or anything else:

_____ minus _____ equals _____
    Sale price   *COGS*   *Gross profit*

Using our watch example, here's how this calculation would look:

Product	Sale price	COGS-Cost of the watch plus freight	Gross profit
Watch #1	$100	$35	$65
Watch #2	$500	$305	$195

5. Multiply the percentage of total sales you want each product to produce (you calculated that in question 2) by the total monthly Administrative expenses (number in question 4), to get the percentage of Administrative expenses that you want each product to cover.

   Example (We'll use 4 different watch models to cover $45,000 of Administrative expenses per month):

   Watch #1: 33% of expenses x $45,000 = $14,850 of the expenses will be covered by this model

   Watch #2: 10% of expenses x $45,000 = $4,500 of the expenses will be covered by this model

   Watch #3: 50% of expenses x $45,000 = $22,500 of the expenses will be covered by this model

   Watch #4: 7% of expenses x $45,000 = $3,150 of the expenses will be covered by this model.

   Check your math this way: The total percentages of expenses covered must equal 100%, and the total expense numbers added up (in our example above, $14,850 plus $4,500 plus $22,500 plus $3,150) must equal the total monthly Administrative expenses (in our case, $45,000).

6. Take your Gross Profit per item amount from question 4 above and divide it into your Administrative expenses from question 5 above.

Monthly administrative expenses per item	number from #4
Divided by the gross profit per item sold	÷answer from #5
Equals the quantity of this item you need	= number of items
to sell to break even, per month	to break even

Here's the watch example again:

Watch #1 should cover 33% of the total Monthly Administrative Expenses, which equals $45,000 X 33% = $14,850 of the total Monthly Administrative Expenses.

Monthly administrative expenses	$14,850
Divided by the gross profit per watch	÷$70
Equals the number of watches that must be sold to cover 33% of the administrative expenses (actually it's 212.14, but we have to round up because we can't sell a fraction of a watch).	= 213

Whew. Give yourself a huge pat on the back for wading through this. Even though this might have been hard, you now have some extremely valuable information that can make the difference between life and death in your business. Okay, maybe not life and death, but between sleeping well at night and waking up in a cold sweat.

BREAK-EVEN CALCULATION QUESTIONS FOR SERVICES

Use this if you only sell services by the hour.

1. Go back and get your "Total All non-COGS Expenses" you forecasted for month one from the next to the bottom row of the chart on page 144. Write that number here: _____

2. Write your hourly billable rate here: _____

3. Divide the total expenses in month one by your hourly rate.

4. Equals the number of hours you have to bill to break even in month one. Write that number here: _____

Example:

Monthly admin expenses for a CPA practice	**$12,000 per month**
Divided by the CPA's hourly rate	**÷$200 per hour**
Equals 60 hours/month to break even	**= 60 hours**

Now do the same calculation for every other month. (Unless your expenses are the same every month, in which case, You're Done.) You now know how many hours you need to bill every month.

BREAK-EVEN CALCULATION QUESTIONS FOR PRODUCTS AND SERVICES

Use this if you sell products and services.

1. Go back and get the total expenses you forecasted for month one from the "Total All non-COGS Expenses" line from the chart on page 156. Write that number here: _____

2. Go back and get the Gross Profit you forecasted for month one from selling your products, from the "Gross Profit" line from the chart on page 152. Write that number here:_____

3. Subtract your total expenses for month one (the number in question 1) from your Gross Profit (number in question 2). Write that number here: _____

4. Write your hourly billable rate here: _____

   Divide the number you calculated in question 3 (expenses left to cover by your services) by your hourly billable rate.

   Equals the number of hours you have to bill to break even in month one. Write that number here: _____

   Example: A landscaping business that sells plants (products) and installation (services):

   This business has $10,000 of General and Administrative expenses per month. It earns $2,000 per month on the sale of plants and trees. Therefore, the installation services must cover the other $8,000 of expenses (because $10,000 – $2,000 = $8,000).

If you bill installation at $25/hour, you must bill 320 hours/month to break even:

Amount of monthly expenses to cover	$8,000 of expenses
Divided by the hourly billable rate	÷ $25 per hour
Equals the number of hours that need to be billed per month to break even	= 320 hours per month

(Hopefully, it's obvious that you can't work 320 hours per month by yourself. This is at least two people working pretty hard.)

5. Now do the same calculation for every other month. (Unless your expenses are the same every month, in which case, You're Done. Yahoo!)

You now know how many hours you need to bill in a month, and how much product you need to sell, to break even. Now go out and sell *more* than you have calculated. Remember, breaking even isn't the goal. Making a profit is the goal.

Bonus Section #2
CASH FLOW

Now that you've done your income and expense forecasts, you may have noticed a question trying to get your attention, especially if your clients don't pay you right on the spot.

What about cash flow? What if I don't get paid five minutes after I make the sale, deliver the service, sell the product?

What you just did was forecast your income using an underlying assumption that I didn't point out: that the income would be received when you make the sale. This may not be true for you. In fact, chances are good you have to wait for your money for 30 days (or longer).

If you do have to wait for your money, that means you have Receivables. Receivables (the full name is, Accounts Receivable) are monies people owe you because you've delivered a product or service to them, but they have not yet paid you.

Receivables are monies due to you, but not yet collected. This is the crucial difference between them and cash. You can buy things with cash, but it's more difficult (not impossible, but difficult, and usually expensive) to buy things with receivables.

For that reason, it's very important to track your income (the sales you have made) *and* your receivables (the money you've earned but not yet been paid). Separately. Even better, get one person to focus on generating and closing sales (that might be you, the business owner), and get someone else to focus on collecting the receivables (like your bookkeeper or CPA or office manager). This can help the person generating the sales focus on his job and not get distracted by issues around collecting the money.

Let's go back to our original issue: you aren't collecting your money in the same month as you sell your products or services. In the meantime, your landlord (the utility company, the phone company, or anyone else you owe money to) isn't interested that you don't get paid in the same month you make the sale. They want the January bills paid in January.

If you get paid more than 15 days after you finalize your sale or deliver your service, you must take this delay into consideration.

I'm going to give you an example, then give you space to calculate your own cash flow.

We'll use a shirt company as an illustration first.

This is their forecast, assuming they get paid the same month they make the sale:

	January	February	March
Shirt sales (1,000 per month at $100 per shirt)	$100,000	$100,000	$100,000
Cost of shirts (at $30 per shirt)	$30,000	$30,000	$30,000
Freight ($5 per shirt)	$5,000	$5,000	$5,000
Total COGS	$35,000	$35,000	$35,000
Total gross profit	$65,000	$65,000	$65,000
Admin expenses	$45,000	$45,000	$45,000
Net profit	$20,000	$20,000	$20,000

Now look what happens if they have to pay for the shirts up front, but they don't get paid for the shirts until 30 days after they're sold.

	January	February	March
Shirt sales (1,000 per month at $100 per shirt) *Note,* they sold the shirts in January, but won't collect the money until February, so this figure is 0 in the first month	0	$100,000	$100,000
Cost of shirts (at $30 per shirt)	$30,000	$30,000	$30,000
Freight ($5 per shirt)	$5,000	$5,000	$5,000
Total COGS	$35,000	$35,000	$35,000
Total gross profit	−$35,000	$65,000	$65,000
Admin expenses	$45,000	$45,000	$45,000
Net profit	−$80,000	$20,000	$20,000

Uh oh. They lost $80,000 the first month because they had expenses, but no revenue to cover them. The revenue will come in the next month, but their vendors want to be paid in the month they deliver the shirts: the freight company wants its money when the shirts are delivered, and the employees want to get paid regardless of when the company receives its money. This company has to come up with a solution to this cash shortfall.

Now let's calculate your cash flow.

1. What is the average lag time (number of days) between when you make a sale and when you get paid? Fill in the number of days here: _____

2. Using the chart below, move the income you forecasted into the month where you'll actually get paid. What happened?

	Month					
	1	2	3	4	5	6
Put the cash you receive in the line, under the month you actually collect it						
Put your total expenses here						
Subtract the cash you collect from the expenses and put the result in this row						

Are there any negative numbers in the third row? If so, you have to address your cash-flow issues.

Here are some ways to handle this:

1. Negotiate payment terms with your vendors so you don't have to pay them until you get paid. Many vendors will give you thirty-day terms (i.e., they deliver the product or service to you now, and you pay them in 30 days).

2. Get some money in the bank before you start your business. You'd be surprised at how many people have to close their doors because of cash flow issues. The business may be profitable, but the cash doesn't show up on time, so the business closes.

3. Negotiate a loan, secured by your Accounts Receivable, from your bank. This means that the bank would loan you money to cover the $80,000 shortfall illustrated above, and as your clients pay for the shirts, you pay the bank back. If anything bad happens, the bank will get its money from the clients who owe you the money.

4. Make your clients pay you up front, or even in advance of service. Many coaches, attorneys, CPAs and other people who work by the hour do this. Almost all Internet retailers charge your debit card the second the merchandise leaves the warehouse.

5. Is there a way to start your business on a smaller scale, and keep your day-job longer, without working yourself to death?

People often use credit cards to cover shortfalls like this. I don't recommend it. Here's why:

First, it's very easy and tempting to get into financial trouble with credit cards. You can miss a payment and cause the interest rate to jump to exorbitant heights. In the bad old days, I was late on two payments on one of my credit cards and the interest rate "adjusted" to 28 percent.

Ouch. You can fool yourself into thinking that "paying" for something with a credit card means you actually did "pay" for it (false). You can let the fact that you have credit remaining on a card lull you into not paying attention to your real cash flow.

Second, unless you pay your balances off every month, the interest you pay on your credit cards can mount astronomically. Consider the example of someone who "buys" new office furniture for $2,000 by putting it on a credit card that charges 18% interest. If our hapless consumer pays the $40 minimum payment every month, it will take 30 years to pay off the $2,000, and she will have paid the credit card company an additional $5,000 in interest! I hope this example alone is enough to make you think twice about using credit cards.

Third, using credit cards can create a fog of vagueness in your business numbers. Some business owners charge all their business expenses on a credit card, and then pay it off every month. If you don't go the extra step and re-allocate all your expenses out of the credit card statement and into your bookkeeping program, you'll create the delusion that your biggest business expense is MasterCard or Visa. Lack of clarity on numbers has killed millions of businesses. Don't let yours be one of them.

You hear the romantic stories about how people financed their wonderful, successful businesses (or made movies) with credit cards, but you don't hear so much about the bankruptcies that happen when people get in over their heads (although lately, that's changing). I know you can get lots of frequent flyer miles and other goodies. I'm just recommending you look at the total cost and risks of using credit cards before you employ them in your business.

The Numbers

WHAT ARE YOUR KEY MEASUREMENTS?

In the business world, the rearview mirror is always clearer than the windshield.

WARREN BUFFETT

The third part of the numbers work is figuring out what the two or three key measurements are that must be watched to make sure your business stays profitable.

Your business has a few (less than five) key measurements that you need to monitor every week, sometimes every day, or even every hour.

They tell you how the business is doing. Really efficient key measurements can forecast your cash flow 15, 30, even 60 days out. If you want to learn a little corporate-speak, you can call these key measurements "KPIs," which stands for "key performance indicators."

For example, in many service businesses, (attorneys, CPAs, computer network installers, plumbers) work is billed by the hour. So one obvious key measurement is: *what percentage of their time was spent doing work that is billable to the client?* Some CPA firms expect their employees to be 90% billable; that is, out of a 40-hour work week, 36 hours of work had better be billed to the client.

What's the other key measurement in this scenario? It's the *average dollar amount that the client is paying.* In this example, the CPA might be billing 36 hours a week to his client, but if the client is only paying $10 per hour, no matter how many hours the CPA bills in a week, he'll never make enough money. The *billable rate* is too low.

So the two key measurements in this example are *billable percentage* and *billable rate.*

Let's look at another example: businesses that make things, like cabinet makers, architects, engineers, framers, dry-wall installers, and other construction companies.

The first key measurement for this group is: how close are my estimates of the time, and the materials I thought I would use, compared to the time and materials the job actually took? In other words, *how close are my estimates to real life?* You can see that this measurement is absolutely crucial. If you are charging the customer based on your estimates and, your estimates are low, you will soon underestimate your way out of business.

A second less obvious measurement here is: *how often are you called back to fix something once you finish it?* Pulling your crew(s) or your own self off the next job to go back and fix something at the previous job is painfully expensive and can make for an upset client, or ten.

Let's look at another kind of business: retail stores. Their primary key measurement is what's called *"inventory turnover."* This measures how many times all your merchandise is sold over the course of a year. So if you bought $100,000 worth of goods into your store, and you sold $100,000 worth during the whole year, your inventory "turned" once. There are books and Web sites that tell you what the inventory turns should be for your particular type of store.

You can also create a key measurement to help you track your sales or marketing activity. If you know that if you talk to 50 live people per month, your sales come in at the rate your need them to, then your key measurement is *how many times did I pick up the phone and call people today?* If you have to talk to 50 people per month, perhaps a way to implement your key measurement would be to have three conversations with people per day, even if that means dialing the phone ten or fifteen times to actually talk to three people.

In this same vein, you could measure *how many e-mail newsletters you send out,* or *how many networking events you attend,* or *how many blog entries you write,* or *how many flyers you mail to your prospect list.*

You want to measure the crucial activities that produce prospects and/or sales for your business, whatever they are.

There are other key measurements that, even though they have nothing directly to do with revenue or expenses, can be highly useful in predicting your future success.

You want to measure the crucial activities that produce prospects and/or sales for your business, whatever they are.

A perfect example is *customer satisfaction*. You could create a survey that would ask customers about their level of happiness with your service and produce a number from their responses. Perhaps you would shoot for "90% of our customers are either satisfied or very satisfied with our work." You could track this monthly, quarterly, or even yearly. Even though the measurement of customer satisfaction isn't directly related to revenue or expense, it will still predict profitability. You might not feel the effects of happy customers (or unhappy ones!) immediately, but you certainly will over the long haul.

Every business can benefit from measuring customer satisfaction. There are easy-to-use (and virtually free) e-mail survey systems that you can use to ask your clients how you're doing.

Another possible key measurement is *repeat business*. If your business thrives on customers coming back to you over and over, how will you measure whether they are indeed returning?

The good news about measuring things is that the information you get back helps you adapt to what's working for your customers, what's working in your marketing, and what's working with your prices. If you are the kind of business that has to bid on work; as you track your estimates against reality, the information you get will help you make more accurate estimates. The people who charge by the hour get to see if it is really possible to do client/billable work 90% of the time. Retail stores get to see how popular their merchandise really is.

In the case of our cold caller; if you continue to make 50 calls per month and your sales increase, you might get to generate more profit in your business. Or, if your sales decrease even though you're making your calls, you might need to consider changing your marketing strategy: who you're calling, how many people you're calling, or if cold calling still works in your marketplace.

People say "the devil is in the details." In our case, I think the soul of our businesses is in the details. There is so much information you can glean about your business by measuring a few key items, it makes sense to get moving on this right away. If you think about your business as a servant, that it exists to serve your clients (and you), looking at your key measurements is the best way to see if your business is doing its job the way you want it to.

It is possible to make this highly complex, but if you do that, the measuring and reporting won't get done. The idea is to choose two or three key measurements that you can easily look at (preferably via a computer generated report), then look at these measurements frequently.

A final note. The ultimate key measurement is, "Am I Making Enough Money?" First of all, if you aren't already paying attention to this, your bookkeeper, CPA, and banker will force you to. Secondly, though, this measurement isn't all that useful in helping you take action right now. It doesn't predict the future, it just reports the past.

If you aren't making enough money, by the time you run your income statement at the end of the month and find this out, you've lost 30 days that you could have been taking steps to remedy the problem.

That's why I've listed these other potential key measurements for you, and I encourage you to start using them right away so you can react to changes more quickly.

Swift reaction to change is one of the huge competitive advantages we have as small businesses. The way you can see how things are changing, and make adjustments accordingly, is to stay in constant contact with your clients and customers, and watch your key measurements.

The best key measurements predict the future.

Can you come up with at least one that will help you do that?

If you are working in a group, select another partner (preferably someone you haven't worked with yet), and brainstorm with each other to fill in the grid below. Copy your partner's answers into his book, and have him/her do the same for you.

If you are working with a partner, brainstorm with each other to fill in the grid below. Copy your partner's answers into his book, and have him/her do the same for you.

If you are working alone, fill in the grid below. Then review your key measurements with your CPA or bookkeeper.

Key Measurements

Key measurement Description	How will I get the information?	How often do I need the information?
1.		
2.		
3.		
4. (Optional)		

No matter whether you're working with someone or by yourself, find someone who will listen to you take the Key Measurements Pledge below, and ask them to keep you accountable to your pledge.

I, _____ swear that I will create the report (or delegate this job) to get my key measurements every _____ (day, week, month, quarter). I will report these key measurements, along with my monthly income and expenses to my _____ (CPA, Partner, Sales Force, Coach) every _____ .

Signed: _____

Date: _____

Once you are satisfied with your Key Measurements, transfer them to the Passion, Plan, Profit Business Plan Template on page 215.

Clarity

- - - - - - - - - - - -

You made it through the Numbers and almost everything else. Congratulations!

The last module is Goals and Plans.

This module is the final step in creating clarity for yourself. It will help you choose the most powerful actions to take over the next twelve months, make commitments as to when you will start and finish these actions, and help you put them in your calendar so they will actually get done.

If doing the Numbers section flattened you, go back and take a look at your Purpose. Remind yourself why you're in business. You can also look at the People module (Module Five) to remind yourself who you are serving. Your people need you. Keep going.

I hope you've discovered many things that are working well in your business, or are good about your new business idea. This final module is the place to list the things you've discovered that need to be finished, fixed, or changed. This is where you finalize the steps you need to take to make sure you can earn what you need to live a prosperous and abundant life.

Remember that prosperous earning is a vital part of running a successful business.

In this module I will be reminding you not to take on too many projects at once. Entrepreneurs are notorious for starting twenty things and not finishing any of them. I purposely left only enough space for five goals for the year, in addition to your two revenue goals. Pick your top five and focus on finishing them. You can add more as you complete the ones on your list. If you know you excel at starting things but have trouble finishing them, get some finishers on your team. They don't have to be employees; they can be a coach, a CPA, a fellow businessperson, or anyone else you can be accountable to.

You will also be creating tasks for yourself that you will spread throughout the next twelve months. Have your calendar handy so you can enter your them directly into it.

This is the final push. Keep going. You're almost finished.

Goals and Plans

YOUR ROADMAP FOR
THE NEXT 12 MONTHS

> Unless commitment is made, there are only promises
> and hopes . . . but no plans.
>
> PETER DRUCKER

You've spent significant time and brain cells on creating clarity in your business: clarity about your perfect customers, the products and services you want to sell, your numbers, your key measurements.

You may have noticed that there are some things you need to change, to add, to take away, in your business to put this newfound clarity to work. You can take everything you've learned, everything you've realized, everything you want, and create goals for the year to make your vision materialize. That's why I put this section last.

Your first goal is always your total sales for the year. Remember, you forecasted this number in the Vision section (Module Two), and perhaps modified it in the Income Forecast section (Module Nine). The second goal is your taxable salary. You also forecasted this number in the Vision section. I promise this is the last lecture about this, but I can't pass up my final opportunity to repeat: your business *must* pay you an abundant salary (in addition to making a good profit), or you won't be able to serve your Purpose. That's why these numbers are your first two goals.

Here's the paradoxical news about these first two goals. They aren't controllable, which means they violate "Rule Number One" about goalsetting. If you've read any goalsetting books in the last twenty years, you'll remember that one of the characteristics of a "good" goal is that it must be under your control. We set these two goals anyway. Don't argue. Just trust me and do it. There is something magical about putting these numbers down on paper, even if you can't control them.

> Take everything
> you've learned,
> everything you've
> realized, everything
> you want, and create
> goals for the year
> to make your vision
> materialize.

I'm going to require that all the subsequent goals you set are under your control. They will also have action plans under them, which are the steps you will take to make your goals come true. These plans will also have dates; you will commit not just to the goal, but also to when you will finish it.

Where do you look for your goals? Usually business owners have way too many things to do and not enough time. But if you're wondering where to look for your most meaningful goals, here are some suggestions:

1. Go back and look at your Purpose. Are you doing what you say you want to do in your business? Selling the kinds of products, providing the kinds of services that are aligned with your purpose? If not, consider listing the changes you need to make to get in alignment with your Purpose as possible goals for the year. You will experience the most success and feel the most fulfilled in direct proportion to how much time you spend working in the areas where you are most gifted.

2. Look at your Vision for the next 12 months. What's not in place that needs to be? Do you need a new computer system, a new office, a new website? Attributes of your Vision that you want to bring to fruition in the next 12 months make good goals.

3. Look at your Mission. Are you walking your talk? Is everything about your business congruent with your Mission? If you are a financial planner, have you taken your own advice and created a plan for yourself? Do your marketing materials (business card, website, the way you answer the phone, what you wear, and a list of 100 other things) reflect who you are trying to be? If there are incongruities anywhere (you're a personal trainer who needs to get in shape, a hairstylist with a bad color job, a banker who writes bad checks in his personal account), *fix these things*. Put them on your list of goals.

4. Look at your Strengths, Weaknesses, Opportunities, Threats. Are there weaknesses that need to be fixed? Opportunities that need to be seized? Threats that need to be planned for? Strengths that need to be strengthened? Add them to your list.

5. Look at your Values and Strategies. If one of your values is "our people are our most important resource," do you need to change your benefit package or publish an employee handbook that spells out just how important your employees are? If one of your strategies is "clear communication," are all your contracts in writing?

6. Look at your Perfect Clients. Are you communicating with them regularly? Are you providing stellar service and products? Do you need to put a systemized marketing campaign on your list of goals? Do you need to create a way to start talking to new prospects?

7. Look at your Key Measurements. Is there a system in place that will deliver them to you regularly, without muss or fuss? Does this mean a new bookkeeping system, or more training on the one you have? Or something else?

Because of who we are (hardworking, crazy perfectionists), it's easy to make a giant list of goals and never finish any of them. I want you to go back and really look at the work you've done so far to make sure the goals you choose are the right ones. I limited the number of goals you could choose to five, on purpose. If you finish all five, great, add five more. It's much better to finish five than to half-finish eight or nine goals. Try to restrain yourself.

Now let's look at what a "good goal" might be.

Here's the first example. What makes it a good goal is that it's under your control, it has a specific time frame to be done in, and it's measurable (i.e., someone other than you can tell if you actually did it or not).

Goal: Reach 2,000 Prospects in Next 12 Months

Plans:

1. Create a downloadable article that educates prospective new clients about an aspect of business by May 10.

2. Talk to web designer. Post article on website; start collecting email addresses from people who download the article for the newsletter by June 1.

3. Create newsletter text for first two newsletters by July 10

4. Talk to 3 newsletter generating companies to get prices, and understand the process by July 25.

It's much better to finish five than to half-finish eight or nine goals.

MODULE 12

PASSION, PLAN, PROFIT

5. Choose newsletter vendor by August 15.

6. Send first edition of newsletter on September 1.

7. Put on calendar one week after each newsletter sent, to read reports about the results of the newsletter (how many people opened it, how many bouncebacks, unsubscribes, etc.)

8. Schedule writing of newsletter on calendar two weeks before newsletter goes out, for the next 12 months, by October 1.

Here's another example. You discovered in your SWOT analysis that your competitors collect their money up front. You need to start doing that too. The goal is:

Create Up-Front Payment System in 1st Quarter

Plans:

1. Change your contracts to reflect the new upfront payment terms by January 1.

2. Train your employees (and yourself) how to collect money up front by January 15.

3. Announce the changes to your customers (and explain why it's good for them) by February 1.

4. Create a feedback loop to make sure everyone is following the new system by February 15.

Another example might be a goal to address having to redo work that wasn't done right the first time. This might be one of your Strategies that hasn't been fully implemented until now.

The goal would be:

Create System to Drive Re-dos to 1% of All Visits in 30 Days

Plans:

1. Create a system to insure the technician reviews each job before he goes to the customer, to make sure he fully understands the problem and has the appropriate parts, by March 15.

2. Set up a "level two" tech support person to help the field engineer with difficult problems while he's still at the client, by March 21.

3. Set up a feedback system so that someone calls each client after the engineer has completed his work to make sure the client is happy, by March 30.

4. Create a tracking system to monitor the outcome of each on-site visit to measure the redo rate by March 30.

Remember when I said that a goal must also be measurable by an outside person to be effective? Here's what I mean. "Focus more effort on selling" is not measurable, because no one but you can tell what "Focus more effort on selling" actually means. "Make five calls per day to prospects," or "Send out 1,000 newsletters per month," on the other hand, is very measurable, by anyone. When you create your goals, make sure they're measurable, even by a disinterested third party.

You can list many potential goals in the following pages, but when it comes to selecting your top picks, be ruthless. A smaller number of goals, with realistic dates, will serve you best.

If you are working in a group, answer questions 1–8 below on your own, then fill in the worksheets on pages 201–203.

From the possible goals you listed on these three pages, choose the top five goals you want to pursue in the next 12 months. Circle them.

Then sit down with someone in your group (preferably someone you haven't worked with yet) and try to convince him that pursuing these goals is the absolute best use of your time. Heed your partner's feedback. You don't have to agree with him, but listen to his suggestions.

Once you have shared your choices and discussed them with your partner, fill in pages 204–205 where you list your five goals and the plans (steps) you will take to accomplish them.

If you are working in a pair, answer questions 1–8 below on your own, then fill in the worksheets on pages 201–203.

From the possible goals you listed on these three pages, choose the top five goals you want to pursue in the next 12 months. Circle them.

Then sit down with your partner and try to convince him that pursuing these goals is the absolute best use of your time. Heed his feedback. You don't have to agree with him, but listen to his suggestions.

Once you have shared your choices and discussed them with your partner, fill in pages 204–205 where you list your five goals and the plans (steps) you will take to accomplish them.

If you are working alone, answer questions 1–8 below on your own, then fill in the worksheets on pages 201–203.

From the possible goals you listed on these three pages, choose the top five goals you want to pursue in the next 12 months. Circle them.

Then fill in your top five goals on pages 204–205. Review your goals with a trusted advisor: your CPA, coach, or someone else, to get their feedback.

Note to everyone: the grids on pages 201–203 all ask you to estimate what it might cost to implement a goal, and what the financial impact of achieving this goal could have on your business. Knowing how much something might cost to do, plus having an idea about the financial impact a goal could have, is one way to decide whether to pursue it or not.

For example, if you think installing a new bookkeeping system would cost $10,000, but would save your business $20,000 in lost billing, it would make sense to put this goal at the top of the list. Spending $10,000 to get back $20,000 is a great investment. In fact, one way to help increase your profitability is to pick goals that have the most impact on generating revenue.

However, don't worry if you don't know the cost or financial impact. You can estimate it, or simply leave that part blank.

You can also download these templates at www.christystrauch.com/books and fill your information in there.

1. What projects are you putting off that you need to do? Some areas that might need attention are:

   - Research and Development
   - Operations
   - Financial Systems
   - Accounting Systems
   - Lead-Generation (i.e., finding prospects to turn into customers)
   - Website Design and Marketing
   - Technology
   - Sales
   - Marketing

   List any projects you are putting off here:

2. Go back and look at your Purpose, your Vision, and Mission. Are there any goals that need to be on your list that come from this work?

3. Go back and look at your Values and Strategies. Are there any objectives that need to be put into place to keep your business true to them?

4. Go back and look at your Strengths, Weaknesses, Opportunities, and Threats. Are there any goals that need to be put in place in the coming year to take advantage of the existing strengths and opportunities, or to fix the weaknesses and address the threats? Are there things your competitors are doing that you need to do also?

5. Go back and look at your People. How do you talk to them, both the ones who already do business with you, and the ones who would love to do business with you if they just knew who you were? This question should produce at least two goals: your system to create new perfect customers for your goods and services, and your system to communicate how awesome you are to your existing clients. **(In fact, if you don't already have a system to bring in new customers and a way to talk to existing ones, those must be your number one and two goals for the year.)**

6. Go back and look at page xxix. Did you make any notes to yourself that need to be added to your list of possible goals?

7. Now take all your answers to questions 1–6 and enter them as possible goals in the charts on pages 200–201, along with their costs and impact on the business, if you know.

8. Are there any projects you'd love to do that wouldn't necessarily generate revenue but would make your heart sing? Enter them in the grid on page 202.

9. Are there any projects, product lines, services you're doing now that you want to stop? Enter them in the grid on page 203.

10. Now choose your top five projects (these become your Goals for the year) from the previous grids above (include at least one from the "make your heart sing" list) and fill out the table on pages 204–205 with at least three plans (steps) for each goal, and the dates by which you're committing to have them finished. *Note: THERE MUST BE AT LEAST ONE MARKETING PROJECT* (i.e., communicating with your existing clients and new prospects) *ON THIS LIST.* Once you are satisfied with your Goals and Plans, transfer them to the *Passion, Plan, Profit* Business Plan Template on page 215.

11.   Now, on your own, enter the Goals and Plans you listed above on the calendar on page 207. You can transfer this to Outlook or whatever other calendar you use, but put them here first so you can see the entire year and decide if your plans are not ambitious enough, or more likely, too ambitious. It's better to do a few things well than a lot of them badly. Don't forget: if you want to send out a newsletter on March 15, you might have to put some of the preliminary newsletter tasks in January and February. When March 15 rolls around, the newsletter will be ready, and you won't have to stay up the night before to finish it. Post this calendar somewhere so you see it every day.

12. Read page 199. Don't skip this step. It's a small action that will plant both of your feet on the path.

You are almost finished.

You probably have a long list of things to do.

You might feel overwhelmed.

Your saboteur may be sharpening his knives on the back of your neck to get you to stop.

Use this page to write down the ONE THING (it can be very small) that you will do first, beginning tomorrow morning.

The thing I am going to do first:

_____

Tear this piece of paper out of the book (or make a copy of it) and tape it to the inside of your front door.

Do this task you wrote down, first thing tomorrow morning.

Everything will flow from here.

POSSIBLE GOALS

Possible goal	Estimated annual cost	Financial impact to the business

Possible goal	Estimated annual cost	Financial impact to the business

PROJECTS YOU'D LOVE TO DO

Project	Cost to the business	Impact on you and/or the business

PROJECTS/PRODUCTS/SERVICES YOU'D LIKE TO STOP DOING

Project / product line / service	Cost to the business to stop	Impact on you and/or the business

LIST OF FINAL GOALS

Goal	Steps to get going on this goal (plans)	Dates to complete each step
1.	1. 2. 3. 4. 5. 6.	1. 2. 3. 4. 5. 6.
2.	1. 2. 3. 4. 5. 6.	1. 2. 3. 4. 5. 6.
3.	1. 2. 3. 4. 5. 6.	1. 2. 3. 4. 5. 6.

Goal	Steps to get going on this goal (plans)	Dates to complete each step
4.	1. 2. 3. 4. 5. 6.	1. 2. 3. 4. 5. 6.
5.	1. 2. 3. 4. 5. 6.	1. 2. 3. 4. 5. 6.

Example of an Activity Calendar for a Writer/Business Coach

This person has set aside time to do these tasks well in advance of when he wants the final product to appear. For example, he wants to start sending his newsletter in November, so he has scheduled to work on it in October. This gives him time think about it and to do it right, instead of racing around at the last minute. If you're addicted to adrenaline, you won't like planning things in advance, but you'll live a lot longer if you do it this way.

This planning calendar is intended to let you look at the next 12 months and plan your work to achieve your goals in a way that gives you time to think about how to do them right, instead of doing them at the last minute.

Month October	Month November	Month December
Goal #1: Finish edits on first book Plan: Schedule 1 hour writing time/5 days per week starting 10-1	**Goal #1:** Finish edits on first book Plan: 1 hour writing, 5 days/week	**Goal #1:** Finish edits on first book Plan: 1 hour writing, 5 days/week. Send final edited copy to editor by 12-15
Goal #2: Client communication system Plan: Interview and select newsletter company by 10-15 Plan: Write list of possible newsletter topics by 10-31 Plan: Get *Naked Conversations* book and read by 10-31 Plan: Call web designer 10-15, ask them to set up blog by 10-31	**Goal #2:** Client communication system Plan: Start writing newsletter by 11-3, finish by 11-6, get newsletter co. to send it out by 11-15 Plan: Write 5 short blog posts, run them by web designer by 11-6. Post 2 per week starting 11-10	**Goal #2:** Client communication system Plan: Start writing newsletter by 12-3, finish by 12-6, out on 12-15 Plan: Write 5 blog posts on 12-3; 5 more on 12-17; post 2 per week starting 12-4. **Goal #3:** Create teleclass curriculum Plan: Go to coffee shop and think quietly for 3 hours about topics; list 20 possible topics on 12-5

12-MONTH ACTIVITY CALENDAR

Month _____	Month _____	Month _____
Month _____	Month _____	Month _____
Month _____	Month _____	Month _____
Month _____	Month _____	Month _____

You're Done!

Each success only buys an admission ticket to a more difficult problem.

HENRY KISSINGER

But not really. This is just the beginning. In fact, the minute you set all this down on paper, it begins to change. When you look at your business plan next week you'll already notice that things are different than you originally conceived.

Does this make the process less worthwhile or less reliable or less useful? *Absolutely not.*

A useful business plan is just the starting line. Once you start operating in clarity with your numbers, by comparing your actual results to your forecast, you'll see you didn't include some services or products that you didn't even know about. Some of your products may become much more popular and some might fade away.

You'll gain clarity about your best customers, and, using your key measurements, you'll know whether you're making money, how much you're making, and whether your customers are happy. A working business plan is a crucial tool for a profitable business. A good one will lead you through the entire life of your business.

Even if every assumption you made in the workbook turns out to be erroneous, the process is *still* worthwhile. All the information you gather and measure against your original assumptions this year will make for an even better business plan and an even more profitable business, next year. In fact, I have included instructions in Appendix 5 to help you review your plan monthly and quarterly, to make the process of updating your plan easy and quick.

A working business plan is a crucial tool for a profitable business.

This Is What To Do Next:

1. Enter the activities you mapped out for the year into your calendar. Yes, I know I already told you to do this in the Goals module, but just in case you didn't, do it now.

2. Share the plan with your employees/support staff, if you have them. Review your progress against the plan, monthly, with them.

3. Track your actual numbers, monthly, against the forecast you made in this plan. This can be challenging, especially if you are falling short in any areas you forecasted. Do it anyway. The easiest way to do this is to enter the forecast you did in the Income and Expenses modules into your bookkeeping software. The software will have a place to enter a "Budget" for the year, month by month, and by income and expense category. Get your bookkeeper to do this, or type "Budget" into the "help" function of the software and it will walk you through how to do it. Once your forecast is entered into your bookkeeping program, you'll be able to compare your forecast to your actual results by simply printing a report ("Budget vs. Actual") whenever you want.

4. Set a monthly meeting with someone (coach, CPA, bookkeeper, mentor, etc.) and look at how your numbers are actually adding up, versus your forecast. Make adjustments to your forecast as you see how your business is unfolding.

5. Look at your key measurements regularly. The easiest way to do this is to set up your bookkeeping software to produce them automatically. Get your bookkeeper or CPA to help you if you can't figure out how to set this up alone.

6. Get an accountability partner. This is a fancy term for someone you talk to at least twice a month to review your key measurements, your goals and plans, and how things are going in your business. This person needs to be someone with whom you can be completely honest.

   Some ideas are: the person you did this workbook with, if you did it with someone else, your bookkeeper, general manager, CPA, or business coach. Set up your bimonthly meetings with them in advance and *don't cancel them* unless it's life or death.

Writing a business plan, then monitoring your results throughout the year, is what Stephen Covey calls *"Important, Not Urgent"* work. Reviewing the progress on your plan twice a month can make the difference between a decent business and a stellar one. Because your business has a deep purpose in the world, give it every chance to succeed.

Appendixes

THE *PASSION, PLAN, PROFIT* BUSINESS PLAN TEMPLATE

Name of Business _____

Date _____

1. Purpose—Why you are in business:

2. Vision—The Destiny of Your Business (1-year and 3-year)

   Total Revenue for the next 12 months: _____

   My taxable salary for the next 12 months: _____

   One-Year Vision:

   Three-Year Vision:

3. Mission—Your Service to the World (What you tell the world about what you do.)

4. Values—Your Moral Compass

    1.

    2.

    3.

    4.

    5.

5. Target Market—Find Your People, Make Relationships with Them, Help Them Buy

Client type	Description	How to find them	How to make relationships with them	How to help them buy

6. Strategies—Your Business Compass

    1.

    2.

    3.

    4.

    5.

7. Unique Selling Proposition—What makes you different from everyone else?

8. Strengths, Weaknesses, Opportunities, Threats—Your Analysis from the Inside Out:

    Strengths:

    1.

    2.

    3.

    4.

    Weaknesses:

    1.

    2.

    3.

    4.

Opportunities:

1.

2.

3.

4.

Threats:

1.

2.

3.

4.

9. The Numbers—Your Income (see spreadsheet on pages 100–111 or pages 114–125)

10. The Numbers—Your Expenses (see spreadsheets on pages 138–145 or pages 146–157)

11. The Numbers—What are your Key Measurements? (What numbers do you need to watch that will tell you how your business is doing?)

Key Measurement #1: Monthly revenue

Key Measurement #2: Monthly net profit

Key Measurement #3 _____

Key Measurement #4 _____

12 Goals and Plans—Your roadmap for the next twelve months

Goal 1: Sales revenue for the year: _____

Goal 2: Taxable salary for the year: _____

Goal 3: _____

Plan #1:

Plan #2:

Plan #3:

Plan #4:

Plan #5:

Goal 4: _____

Plan #1:

Plan #2:

Plan #3:

Plan #4:

Plan #5:

Goal 5: _____

Plan #1:

Plan #2:

Plan #3:

Plan #4:

Plan #5:

Goal 6: _____

Plan #1:

Plan #2:

Plan #3:

Plan #4:

Plan #5:

Goal 7: _____

Plan #1:

Plan #2:

Plan #3:

Plan #4:

Plan #5:

NOTES

CHECKLIST TO TRACK YOUR BUSINESS PROGRESS

Once your business plan is finished, look at this checklist. It lists actions you need to consider taking as your business grows. Go down the list and make sure you're on track, especially if you have been in business for awhile and you consider yourself to be at the intermediate or advanced level.

Beginning

☐ 1. Separate your business and personal finances in every way. This means separate accounting programs (or at least separate companies/entities in the same software package), separate checking accounts, and separate savings accounts.

☐ 2. Open a business savings account for taxes and deposit 15%–20% of every check you get into the account.

> Go down the list and make sure you're on track.

☐ 3. Open a business savings account for your Business Prudent Reserve (money set aside for unexpected expenses, and to cover temporary downturns in business) and put 10% of every check in there.

☐ 4. Get an accounting program, and get a professional person to set it up for you. Get the person to train you on how to, at the minimum, run your Key Measurements reports from it.

☐ 5. Buy health insurance for yourself.

☐ 6. Open another business savings account for retirement and put *something* in it from every check you get, even if it's only $5. The habit is more important than the amount you deposit. Once you get in the habit of making the deposits, the dollar amount sometimes magically begins to increase.

Yes, I am serious about having three *separate* savings accounts for different purposes. Having savings accounts for separate purposes will help you see, at a glance, how much you have set aside for each of these very important funds, and will help you focus on the fact that your business must fund more than just your rent and the light bill.

Intermediate

☐ 1. Start a *personal* savings account to cover your medical insurance deductible. Call your insurance agent to see if a health savings account makes sense for you.

☐ 2. Buy disability insurance for yourself. Talk to your CPA about whether the business should pay for this or not.

☐ 3. Fund your business savings account for your Prudent Reserve fully (one of the savings accounts you started by following my advice in the beginning). Start by having three months of your business expenses in it, including your salary. Keep going until you have six months of your business expenses in it.

☐ 4. Calculate how much money you need to retire (there are numerous calculators on the Internet that can help you. Type "retirement calculator" into any search engine). Figure out how much money you need to deposit in your retirement account monthly. Adjust your salary if you need to so you can take the retirement deposits out of your salary; increase your marketing to bring in more money; adjust your income forecast accordingly, and begin to make those deposits. I realize I'm making these steps sound easy, especially the "increase your marketing to bring in more money." Figure out what you need for retirement first, then you can draw on what you already know about what works in your business and get help from your support people (CPA, marketing company, coach, etc.) to help you with the rest.

Advanced

☐ 1. Open a (yes another) *personal* savings account for "sick leave and vacation" and gradually accumulate enough money from your salary for you to take six weeks off and take a nice vacation, plus support six weeks of missed income.

☐ 2. Start thinking about a succession plan. Who will take over your business when you retire or want to do something else? There are many exit strategies, from selling your business to a competitor, to family member(s), to your employees, or to a larger company in your niche. Start thinking about which one you want, and begin shaping the business so it can be sold. There are books and resources on the Internet to tell you how to get your business in shape to sell it. The two absolutes are clean, honest bookkeeping, and a marketing program that doesn't depend on you personally, to work.

☐ 3. Have one year of business operating expenses in your business savings account. This will give you enough cushion to let you to experiment with new products and/or services and not have to turn them into moneymakers right from the beginning.

☐ 4. If you love to do the technical work of your business (you have a carpentry business and you like doing the carpentry, you own a beauty salon and you love to cut hair, etc.), have you set your business up so that you can spend the most time doing what you love?

If you don't like the technical work, have you found a way to hire others to do it, and are you spending more of your time working *on*, instead of *in*, your business?

☐ 5. Step back and take a look at how you are spending your time, and whether you're happy with your allocation. If you're not happy, go purchase the book *It's About Time,* by Leslie Keenan (it's on Amazon), and read it. It will show you how to track what you spend time on now, and teach you how to change it if you want to.

RESOURCES

I've listed resources below that correspond to the chapters in the book. Feel free to suggest others; email me at christy@christystrauch. com and I will add them to the downloadable list at www.christystrauch. com/books. This is a list of the most current resources at the time of printing. See www.christystrauch.com/books for the latest version.

Chapters 1, 2, and 3: Purpose, Vision, Mission:

Underpinning your purpose, your mission and vision for your business is you: who you are as a person. Who you are is the source of both your superpowers and your blind spots. Thus, knowing yourself is the foundation for your successful business.

These books will help confirm who you are, what matters to you, what you do well, and what you need to delegate.

The E-Myth Revisited, Michael Gerber. (New York, NY: Harper Business, 2004) Gerber describes the three roles every business needs to be filled: leader, manager of the work, and person who does the work. He suggests that all business owners should eventually serve as the full-time leader. I disagree. The genius of this book is the description of the roles; once you know what they are you can decide which one(s) you're best at, and get help with the others.

It's About Time, Leslie Keenan. (Novato, CA: The Printed Voice, 2003) How to move from unconscious to conscious spending of your time. A vital skill; as a business owner there will always be more work to do than time to do it.

Embracing Our Selves. (Hal and Sidra Stone. Novato, CA: New World Library, 1989) If you want to understand why one part of you wants to write your business plan while another part is mightily resisting, this book will explain why and give you tools to work with all parts.

The Enneagram in Love and Work (Helen Palmer. San Francisco, CA: Harper San Francisco, 1995) If you want to become genuinely conversant with your blind spots, this book will start the conversation. Particularly helpful when you begin noticing that you're repeating behavior that isn't helpful, but struggle to stop.

Please Understand Me II, David Keirsey. (Newport Beach, CA: Prometheus Nemesis Book Company, 1998) Understand your Myers-Briggs type; highly useful, especially to learn if you get energy from being with people, or from being alone. You'll need to know this about yourself to choose the marketing that will work best for you.

StrengthsFinder 2.0, Tom Rath. (New York, NY: Gallup Press, 2007) Either buy this book new so you can use the code inside to take the Clifton StrengthsFinder test, or buy it used and go to the Gallup website and buy the test directly. Currently the code in the book will only give you the results of your top 5 strengths. It's worth paying the whole $50.00 (as of 2020) to get all 34 strengths in order so you can see the ones at the bottom as well as the top. You'll see in black and white what to delegate and what to do yourself.

The War of Art, Steven Pressfield. (New York, NY: Black Irish Entertainment LLC, 2002) Keep this short book close, so you can re-read it to remember that all creative people (yes, that you) face resistance, and there is a simple way out.

Chapter 4: Values

This link: https://www.taproot.com/live-your-core-values-exercise-to-increase-your-success/ will take you to a list of 40 or so possible values, and walk you through narrowing them to your top five. You can create the exercise on your own by looking up a list of values, printing them, picking 15, then letting go of five to get to your top 10, then repeating once more to find your top five. The exercise is important, but using the information you glean from doing the exercise to make difficult decisions is vital to your long term success.

Leadership and Self-Deception, The Arbinger Institute. (Oakland, CA: Barrett Koehler, 2018) This book will show you the true cause of your problems (hint: there's a clue in the title), and how to liberate yourself from them.

Chapter 5: Your People, Chapter 7: Unique Selling Proposition

This is Marketing, Seth Godin. (New York, NY: Portfolio Penguin, 2018) Seth Godin pioneered the idea of asking permission to market to people instead of bombarding them with irrelevant information they didn't ask for or want. Page 257 contains a list of questions to ask about your business and your clients, the answers will steer you toward the impact you want to make (which is what sets you apart from other businesses) and the people you want to help.

Marketing Tools

Tools to help you market online abound; from website templates to customer tracking and email newsletter apps. Right now these tools are popular:

Website design:

- www.squarespace.com
- www.weebly.com
- www.wix.com
- www.wordpress.com

Tracking customer data (this is called Customer Relationship Management or CRM)

- www.hubspot.com

Email newsletters

- www.convertkit.com
- www.mailchimp.com
- www.mailerlite.com

But before you commit to any of these, see what these review sites recommend.

- www.getapp.com
- www.pcmag.com
- www.cnet.com
- www.producthunt.com

The scarce resource in the tech world isn't the apps or the hardware, it's your time, especially when you're starting out or working solo. If you find an app that you learn easily but costs a bit more, if you can, spend the money.

Chapters 6, 8: Strategies and Strengths, Weaknesses, Opportunities and Threats

One Small Step Can Change Your Life, The Kaizen Way, Robert Maurer. (New York, NY: Workman Publishing 2014) Your SWOT analysis and your strategies will point to changes you need to make in your business. This short book will show you how to make incremental changes without antagonizing the part of your brain that reacts negatively to change. These small changes naturally build on each other to produce seismic shifts.

Chapters 9, 10, 11: Numbers

Money Tools

Simplify your income and spending by tracking it using an online tool. Current popular ones are:

- Quickbooks (www.intuit.com)
- Freshbooks (www.freshbooks.com)
- Mint (www.mint.com owned by Intuit)

Mint is free, but that means you and your information are the product Intuit sells to other companies. Still, it's better to start tracking your money, both personal and business, as soon as you can, and if free is what you have the budget for, start there. Also read the reviews on Getapp.com to see what's popular now.

Money Issues

People have three kinds of money issues.

The first is simple ignorance. If you were never taught how to handle money and all you need is information, your resources are endless, and they include this book. You can tell if this is you by your reaction to the information here (or in any other business plan book). If, as you read you say, "Oh, okay. Now I understand," and you can implement what you read immediately, more information is the answer to your problem.

The next is money trauma. Many people fall into this category. You learned that money is the root of all evil, or that rich people are smart and poor people are dumb, or that money will corrupt your creativity, or that you could never support yourself with your creative practice so you shouldn't try, or you hold other beliefs that make earning, saving and spending money highly problematic. I have used parts work with my clients to address these issues. You can do that for yourself by getting the book, *Embracing Ourselves,* by Hal and Sidra Stone. I have also blogged extensively about how to handle this at www.christystrauch. com/blog

There are also some good books about healing mistaken beliefs about money. Here are two:

The Energy of Money, Maria Nemeth. (New York, NY: The Ballantine Publishing Group 1999)

Financial Recovery, Karen McCall. (Novato, CA: New World Library 2011)

The third issue is total powerlessness. No matter how much information you gather, therapy you get, classes you take, coaches you hire, you can't change your behavior. The only way I know to address this is with a 12-Step Program. There are two good ones. Each of these programs has a "Am I A ____" quiz that you can take to diagnose yourself. If this is your situation, both websites will tell you what steps to take next.

- www.debtorsanonymous.org
- www.underearnersanonymous.org

Chapter 12: Goals and Plans

Getting Things Done, David Allen. (New York, NY: Penguin Books 2015) Because I took the StrengthsFinder test, I know that I'm well-endowed with strategy and relationship skills but dramatically lacking in the ability to execute. To implement the brilliant system described in this book, you need execution proficiency. If you know you need help managing the avalanche of ideas and the crush of multiple projects you're trying unsuccessfully to juggle, but you feel like crying when you think about implementing this system, get someone to help you.

First Things First, Stephen R. Covey, A. Roger Merrill, Rebecca R. Merrill. (New York, NY, Free Press 2003) The most useful concept in this book is the difference between important work (urgent or not), and unimportant work. The authors show you how to figure out what parts of your work are important-urgent, or important-not urgent, and how to spend all your time there.

FOOTWORK CALCULATOR

There's a funny secret that people don't talk much about in business. It concerns what you can and can't control in business (and in life, too, but that's another book).

If you have ever worked in a job where you had a sales quota, i.e., an amount you had to sell every month, you might have labored under the impression that you could control whether your customers bought from you or not. At the minimum, your boss tried to get you to buy into this idea.

You've just spent copious amounts of time creating a financial forecast in this workbook that estimates how much you will earn from your customers over the next 12 months. It seems like I'm suggesting that you can control your income somehow by putting it on paper.

The truth is you *cannot control* how much, if, or when, your customers buy from you. Notice I waited to tell you this until the end of the book.

There is hope. You do have control over something, and that is your footwork—the actions you take to help your customers buy. You control the footwork, *not* the outcome of the footwork. So much for the concept of selling that expects the salesperson to force his customer to buy. People buy because they want to; not because they are coerced. We can certainly make it easier for them to decide to buy, however. That's where footwork (more commonly known as "marketing") comes in.

There are many kinds of footwork. You picked some for your business when you completed the "Who Are Your People?" module. I am going to pick two examples: offering workshops and giving speeches, to illustrate how many of each of these actions our example businesses must do to get in front of enough people so a percentage of them will buy. Even though you can't force anyone to buy, if you get in front of enough of the right prospects who need what you do, a percentage of them will.

> You do have control over something, and that is your footwork—the actions you take to help your customers buy.

The question comes down to: how many people do I need to market to, to make the income I need? Note: if you are looking for a great Key Measurement (Module Eleven), this number will do nicely.

The first worksheet below will take you, step by step, through the example of a business that needs to get in front of 85 people a month to "produce" the sales it needs. This hypothetical business is a computer networking firm whose average order size is $10,000. This firm's best clients are all kinds of construction engineers and architects.

The owner enjoys giving speeches to groups of people that include her target market: engineering and architectural associations. Speeches are her footwork. She needs to give three or four speeches a month to audiences of 25 people to produce the sales she wants. She knows this because one of her key measurements is tracking how many people are attracted to her company each time she gives a speech.

Walk through the directions below to see how the owner arrived at these figures.

Directions

(Follow along with the example on page 234 or download the template at www.christystrauch.com/books and fill in your own data):

Step 1 is the amount of revenue the business needs to generate in the next 12 months. This computer networking firm we are using as the example wants to make $250,000 in sales for the year. Your number will come from your Income Forecast in Module Nine.

Step 2 is the average order size for this business. In this example, the average order size is $10,000, which is the average dollar amount of a computer network installation.

Step 3 tells how many orders (at $10,000 each) the business needs to generate $250,000 in sales, which in this case is 25 (250,000/10,000 = 25).

Step 4 asks "How many of these 25 orders will come from existing customers?" Previous experience (and possibly monitoring this number as a Key Measurement from Module 11) says this business gets 5 orders a year from existing clients. If you don't know how many of your orders will come from existing clients, either go back and look at your last year's sales and see if you can figure it out, or use your gut and guess. If you're just starting out and you don't have any clients, the number that goes in this box is zero.

Step 5 calculates how many *new* orders this business needs in the year. This is the total number needed (25) minus the ones from repeat customers (5), leaving 20 orders that the business needs to generate (25 – 5 = 20).

Step 6 calculates how many orders are needed each month, which is the 20 for the year, divided by 12 months (20/12 = 1.7 orders per month).

Step 7 asks how many *interested* people have to be given quotes before someone actually buys. This business has to talk to 5 interested people before one buys.

Step 8 multiplies the number of actual orders the business needs to get in one month by the number of people needed to have expressed interest in the product, to calculate how many people have to be contacted in the month (1.7 x 5 = 8.5)

Step 9 asks how many new people have to be contacted to find one who wants a quote. This business talks to 10 new people to find one person who is interested in a computer network.

Step 10 says if the business has to give out 8.5 quotes every month to find 1.7 customers who will actually buy, and has to talk to 10 people to find one who is interested in receiving a quote, how many people does the owner need to talk to, to find the 8.5 people who will ask for a quote?" The answer is 8.5 x 10 = 85 people.

Conclusion

This business must market to 85 new people each month (i.e., give speeches to a total of 85 people per month) to get 8.5 people to request a quote, to get 1.7 of them to buy, to make $17,000 per month (plus the other $50,000/year of business that will come straight from referrals), to earn $250,000 in revenue for the year.

FOOTWORK CALCULATOR EXAMPLE —COMPUTER NETWORKING FIRM

Information	The number	Get the number from:
Step 1 Annual sales target	$250,000	Income forecast (Module 9)
Step 2 Average order size	$10,000	Previous experience
Step 3 Orders (or customers/clients) needed each year	25	Step 1 ÷ Step 2
Step 4 Orders/clients which should come from repeat business	5	Previous experience
Step 5 New orders/clients needed in the year	20	Step 3 – Step 4
Step 6 Orders/clients needed each month	1.7	Step 5 ÷ 12 (the number of months in a year)
Step 7 "Conversion rate"—how many quotes given to new prospects become orders	5	Previous experience
Step 8 Number of quotes that must be given each month	8.5	Step 6 x Step 7
Step 9 "Conversion rate"—How many potential customers you contact result in someone asking for a quote	10	Previous experience
Step 10 Potential customers you need to contact (talk to, email, speak to, give workshops to, etc.) each month. **This is your footwork.**	85	Step 8 x Step 9

Our second example is an organizational development coach who finds his clients through giving three-hour workshops. This coach knows that if he gives one workshop a month that follows this formula, he will hit the annual income target he forecasted in Module Nine. He is lucky. He charges for his footwork: people pay $95 each to attend his monthly workshops.

If you want to charge money for your footwork, make sure people glean considerable value from it. It would be possible for the previous example of the owner who gives speeches to charge for her footwork also (i.e., charge for the speeches she gives), but her speeches better deliver significant worth to the audience or the plan will backfire. See the next page for the way the footwork calculator works in this situation.

FOOTWORK CALCULATOR EXAMPLE—
ORGANIZATIONAL DEVELOPMENT COACH

Information	The number	Get the number from:
Step 1 Annual sales target	$150,000	Income forecast (Module 9)
Step 2 Average order size (in this case, the average amount each client spends on coaching with him per year)	$5,000	Previous experience (can come from a Key Measurement—Module 11)
Step 3 Orders (i.e., clients)needed each year	30	Step 1 ÷ Step 2
Step 4 Clients who should come from repeat business (people who come back to him for additional coaching)	5	Previous experience (Key Measurement)
Step 5 New clients needed in the year	25	Step 3 – Step 4
Step 6 New clients needed each month	2.1	Step 5 ÷ 12 (the number of months in a year)
Step 7 "Conversion rate"—how many new people have to be invited to a workshop to get one person signed up for coaching	4	Previous experience (Key Measurement)
Step 8 Number of people who need to show up to each workshop	8.5	Step 6 x Step 7
Step 9 "Conversion rate"—How many potential clients must be contacted to get one person to attend the workshop?	5	Previous experience (Key Measurement)
Step 10 Potential workshop attendees who must be contacted each month	42	Step 8 x Step 9

YOUR FOOTWORK CALCULATOR WORKSHEET

Now fill out this table for your own business:

Information	The number	Get the number from:
Step 1 Annual sales target		Income forecast (Module 9)
Step 2 Average order size		Previous experience
Step 3 Orders (or customers/clients) needed each year		Step 1 ÷ Step 2
Step 4 Orders/clients which should come from repeat business		Previous experience
Step 5 New orders/clients needed in the year		Step 3 – Step 4
Step 6 Orders/clients needed each month		Step 5 ÷ 12 (the number of months in a year)
Step 7 "Conversion rate"—how many quotes given to new prospects become orders		Previous experience
Step 8 Number of quotes that must be given each month		Step 6 x Step 7
Step 9 "Conversion rate"—How many potential customers you contact result in someone asking for a quote		Previous experience
Step 10 Potential customers you need to contact (talk to, email, speak to, give workshops to, etc.) each month. **This is your footwork**.		Step 8 x Step 9

BUSINESS PLAN REVIEW PROCESSES

One of the facts that gives business plans a bad name is that things immediately begin to change right after you finish all your hard work. This makes the plan you worked so diligently on, slowly become outdated and ultimately (I *really* hate to say this), irrelevant.

I have experienced this irrelevance in my own business plan. After I finished my first one, I did review at least the income and expenses for the first couple of months. I had forecasted some large income numbers (sort of like a cross between wishful thinking and everything in the universe needing to line up perfectly in harmony), and I saw that I wasn't making the money I had forecasted in my plan.

Instead of taking this shortfall in as information and making adjustments either to my work or my forecast, I decided to ignore my plan altogether.

Turns out I was not alone in deciding to ignore my plan instead of simply changing it. Almost every person who completed a plan in one of my workshops did the same thing. Evidently we all thought that once the business plan was written, we had better do exactly what we said we would do in the plan, no matter what happened in the outside world.

And if we couldn't do exactly what we planned, then we had better not admit that. Better to simply ignore the plan altogether. Somehow the business plan turned into "an authority figure" who was disappointed in us if we didn't do exactly what we said we would.

Doing and having a business plan was of great help to me. It gave me awareness about what my underlying purpose for being in business really was; it showed me which of my products and services earned the most revenue, it forced me to articulate what was different about my business than others offering the same services, and in general, gave me great clarity. However, it would have been much more helpful to me, had I continued to review it.

I realized that we all needed a review process to keep our plans current, and to counteract this weird transformation that the business plan underwent, from helpful tool to, well, critical parent.

That's what I've put together on the subsequent pages. There are two processes: the monthly review and the quarterly review.

The monthly review will take less than 30 minutes, especially if you have already loaded your income and expense forecast into your bookkeeping software and can run the "Budget vs. Actual" report at the end of every month. The quarterly review will take a little longer. I have included a list of questions you can ask yourself, plus a process for updating the plan so your review can go as smoothly as possible.

Each process will require you to gather some information, and then analyze it. I'll give you the list of information to gather first, then the questions to ask yourself once you've got the information in front of you.

Creating a business plan is not an exercise in foretelling the future. You don't get an A for guessing right. Creating a business plan is an exercise in clarifying your thoughts and guiding your actions based on what you know today. What you will know next quarter will be different.

When that time comes, you will redo your plan to clarify your thoughts and guide your actions for the quarter to come.

Once you have your business plan, the review process will do more to insure your success than almost anything else (except systematic, effective marketing . . . but that's the next book).

If you haven't already, schedule your reviews for next twelve months on your calendar, and honor the appointments as if you had committed to meeting the high school teacher who changed your life, the person you adore who helped you get started in your business, your mentor, or your mother. It's that important.

THE MONTHLY REVIEW PROCESS

Information to gather for the monthly review:

1. Run the Budget vs. Actual report in your bookkeeping software for the month just ended.

    If you don't use bookkeeping software, you can do the same thing by hand. Add up all your sales, preferably by product and/or service, so you can see how much of each thing is selling. Then add up all your expenses in each category. Then get out your income and expense forecast (look up the work you did in Modules Nine and Ten) and compare what you forecasted would happen against what actually did happen.

2. Make a list of your key measurements (from Module Eleven). These measurements should also be listed in the *Passion, Plan, Profit* Business Plan template you filled out as you completed your plan.

3. Get out your Goals and Plans (from Module Twelve). These should also be listed in the Business Plan template.

Analysis of the Information

Write the answers to the questions below in the space below each question. You will use your answers to make changes in your business plan at the end of the review process.

1. Look at your sales, product by product, and/or service by service. Did you sell as much of each as you thought? If the answer is yes, Hurrah for you! Move to the next product/service until you've looked at the sales figures for each one and compared them to what you forecasted when you did your plan.

    Unless you see *radical* as well as unexpected change in any of the sales numbers, it's usually better to wait before taking drastic action. Over three months you can see if the change is a blip, or part of a real trend. That said, pay attention to your gut as you look at your sales numbers and answer the questions below. If, as you answer these questions, your gut is telling you that you need to change something now and not wait for two more months, pay attention.

Pay attention to your gut as you look at your sales numbers and answer the questions below

Note any changes between your forecast and actual sales in the space below.

2. Now let's take a specific look at any of the products or services that brought in less than your forecast. Ask yourself these questions for each product/service that came in lower than you expected:

Is this a seasonal change that happens every year?

Is this a trend that began last month or the month before?

Do you need to take action this month, or wait another 30 days to get more information?

3. If you think you need to take action, review the marketing you're doing for this product/service. Ask yourself these questions:

Did you actually do the marketing for this specific product or service this month?

If you did do the marketing, did you do enough of it?

If you did enough marketing, do you need to change the marketing you're doing?

4. If your sales are much higher than you forecast for any product or service, ask yourself these questions:

    Should you shift your efforts and marketing dollars over to the product(s)/service(s) that are the most successful and stop spending as much time and effort on the ones not meeting their forecasted numbers?

    Do you have enough infrastructure (employees, your own time, outside contractors, raw materials, etc.) to meet the increased demand?

    Note: Sometimes it's difficult to know when to let go of a product or service that's not selling and focus on ones that are. There is no magic answer to this, especially if the trend is relatively new. But you can ask yourself: if you took the time and the marketing dollars away from the low performer and applied it to your star(s), could you estimate what the increase in revenue might be? If the potential new revenue based on spending more time and marketing dollars is significant, does that mean it's time to let go of the low performer?

    If you are reluctant to let go of the under-performer, you can ask yourself these questions: Is it because you are emotionally attached to it? Is it something you really love to do or sell? Is it a product or service that forms part of your purpose for being in business, or does it just feel that way?

If you think you should let go of this under-performer but you don't want to, explore why. It may be a legitimate business decision to stick with it, or you might be deluding yourself. Only you can answer this question.

5. Next, look at your real expenses for the month and compare them to your forecast. Is anything noticeably out of whack (more than 10% different than what you expected)? If so, note the categories that deviated from your forecast in the space below, and any actions you will take to address the issue(s).

6. Now look at your key measurements (from Module Eleven). Are they on track?

   If one of your key measurements shows that sales are down, review your answers to questions 2 and 3 on the previous page and decide if it's time to make some changes, or wait to see what happens in the next month.

   If your key measurements are showing increased sales, review your answer to question 4 on the previous page and decide if you need to make changes.

7. Finally, look at your Goals and Plans. Ask yourself these questions: Did you achieve the goals you set for yourself this month?

   Do you need to put new or different goals and plans on your schedule to take into account any changes in sales this month?

8. Now, based on the answers to these questions, take the following actions:

   A. Change your marketing to respond to higher or lower sales of any of your products/services.

   B. Re-do your income forecast to reflect changes you see happening with your sales. You could raise the amount you have forecasted on the products and services that are doing well, lower the forecast on the ones that aren't, or don't change anything and wait to see what the next month brings.

   C. Re-do your expense forecast to reflect changes you see happening. Have any costs gone up or down significantly? If you think these changes might be permanent, you can alter your expense forecast to bring it more in line with reality.

   D. If you decide to change any numbers in your forecast, make sure you add everything up again to verify that your business will make a profit in the coming month. If you aren't forecasting a profit for the coming month, do you have a business savings account to cover the shortfall? Do you need to take action now (more marketing, greater emphasis on sales, or cutting costs) to insure you can make a profit?

9. Finally, set aside time on your calendar to work on your new goals and plans for the coming month. Don't forget to schedule 30 minutes at the end of the next month to do your month-end review, or 90 minutes at the end of next month if it's time to review the whole quarter.

MONTHLY REVIEW EXAMPLE

On the next page is an example of a monthly review in a CPA firm, where there are two partners, two associates, and things are going well. The first three questions ask you to gather information; we will analyze that information in the subsequent questions.

1   Run the Budget vs. Actual report in your bookkeeping software for the month just ended:

Here's the report from their accounting software.

Note: since you're getting so good at doing the numbers, you're probably curious about how to calculate percent billable time. There are, on average, 176 work hours in a month. Since there are two associates and two partners, there are 352 possible billable hours for each group. Since the partners billed 349 out of a possible 352 billable hours, you can see they billed almost every work hour, hence they were 99% billable (also very tired). The rest of the percentages are calculated the same way.

2.   Make a list of your key measurements (from Module Eleven). These measurements should also be listed in the Passion, Plan, Profit Business Plan template you filled out as you completed your plan. In this case, the CPA firm tracks the following actual numbers and compares them to their forecast:

- **Total revenue billed for the month by associates and partners.**
- **The average hourly rate charged by both associates and partners.**
- **The billable percentage (what percent of their 40-hour workweek was billable to the client?) of the partners and associates**
- **The payroll expenses for both associates and partners.**
- **The total monthly expenses for the office, in addition to payroll for the partners and associates.**
- **Net profit for the month.**

MONTHLY REVIEW EXAMPLE

	January forecast	January actual	Difference
# of hours billed by partners	317 hours	349 hours	32 hours
# of hours billed by associates	334 hours	290 hours	−44 hours
Partner revenue	$63,400	$69,800	$6,400
Associate revenue	$33,440	$29,000	−$4,440
Total revenue	**$96,840**	**$98,800**	**$1,960**
Partner average hourly rate	$200.00	$200.00	$ 0
Associate average hourly rate	$100.00	$100.00	$ 0
Partner percent billable	90%	99%	9% over target
Associate percent billable	95%	82%	13% under target
Payroll-partners	$24,000	$24,000	$ 0
Payroll-associates	$15,120	$14,400	−$720
Total payroll expense	**$39,120**	**$38,400**	**−$720**
General/admin/other expenses	$27,000	$23,562	−$3,438
Net profit for the month	**$30,720**	**$36,838**	**$6,118**

3. Get out your Goals and Plans for the month (from Module Twelve). According to their January goals, they wanted to do the following:

Goal: Gear up for tax season

Plan #1: Make sure all computers and software are updated; replace any that are old or not working.

Plan #2: Make sure the firm has all the new tax preparation software installed on their network.

Plan #3: Make sure everyone is trained on the software.

Plan #4: Check to see how many tax planning handouts they've received back from last year's clients; call the ones who haven't responded.

4. Look at your sales, product by product, and/or service by service.

Looking at the numbers on the spreadsheet, the revenue generated (and the number of hours billed) by the partners exceeded the forecast, while the reverse was true for the associates. This might mean many different things. They could start by asking the associates some questions: did they have enough work to do, did they have questions about the work that didn't get answered, or do the associates have another idea about what caused the discrepancy (since we know no accountant, associate or not, has ever slacked off)?

It might be worthwhile for the partners to look at their performance. Ninety-nine percent billable is very high and made the firm extra money this month, but is it sustainable? Should the partners be delegating more to the associates? Do the associates need more training? Are the tax returns that came in, in January, more complex than ones that will come in later in the year? What is causing such a high billable rate, so early in tax season? These are all questions that need to be answered, based on the number of hours billed.

5. Now let's take a specific look at any of the products or services that brought in less than your forecast. Ask yourself these questions for each product/service that came in lower than you expected:

    Is this a seasonal change that happens every year?

    Is this a trend that began last month or the month before?

    Do you need to take action this month, or wait another 30 days to get more information?

    We already know that the associates billed less than the forecast. The partners have a list of questions to ask, to figure out why this happened. The variation between what was forecasted and what actually happened isn't huge, so the firm might decide to wait another 30 days to see if the trend persists.

    They might also decide to investigate further now, since this business is very seasonal, and they're entering their busy season. It might be good to fix the problem now (or at least figure out if there is a problem), rather than have it get worse when the firm is even busier in the next couple of months.

6. If you think you need to take action, review the marketing you're doing for this product/service. Ask yourself these questions:

    Did you actually do the marketing for this specific product or service this month?

    If you did do the marketing, did you do enough of it?

    If you did enough marketing, do you need to change the marketing you're doing?

    Sales are up in this firm; this month they don't need more sales; they need to figure out how to distribute the work more equitably.

7. If your sales are much higher than you forecast for any product or service, ask yourself these questions:

    Should you shift your efforts and marketing dollars over to the product(s)/service(s) that are the most successful and stop spending as much time and effort on the ones not meeting their forecasted numbers?

Do you have enough infrastructure (employees, your own time, outside contractors, raw materials, etc.) to meet the increased demand?

The partners were 99% billable in January, which might be difficult to sustain over multiple months. Plus, this is just the beginning of their busy season. This might mean that the CPA firm needs to start looking for contract accountants, or even consider hiring someone soon; or run the risk of not being able to serve all their clients before the tax deadline.

8. Next, look at your real expenses for the month and compare them to your forecast. Is anything noticeably out of whack (more than 10% different than what you expected)? If so, note the categories that deviated from your forecast in the space below, and any actions you will take to address the issue(s).

Interestingly, even though the associates were less billable than expected, their payroll expenses were higher. The firm needs to in vestigate what caused the higher payroll expense. Did the associates get paid overtime? If so, why wasn't their billable rate higher?

Additionally, general and administrative expenses were a lot lower than forecasted. The firm can compare these expenses line by line with last month's and last year's at the same time, to see where the discrepancies are. All accounting software packages can create reports to show this comparison.

9. Now look at your key measurements (from Module Eleven). Are they on track?

The firm's key measurements listed on page 247 are on track, with the exceptions we've already discussed in the questions above.

10. Finally, look at your Goals and Plans. Ask yourself these questions:

Did you achieve the goals you set for yourself this month? Do you need to put new or different goals and plans on your schedule to take into account any changes in sales this month?

The firm focused hard on completing the Goals and Plans it set for itself. The partners knew that the computer system had to be ready for tax season, and they have taken the steps to make sure it is.

In fact, they have received 95% of the tax planning documents they sent out to their potential clients, (which is up from 92% last year), they know that the workload will increase and they will need to plan for more business.

11. Now, based on the answers to these questions, take the following actions:

    A. Change your marketing to respond to higher or lower sales of any of your products/services.

    B. Re-do your income forecast to reflect changes you see happening with you sales. You could raise the amount you have forecasted on the products and services that are doing well, lower the forecast on the ones that aren't, or don't change anything and wait to see what the next month brings.

    C. Re-do your expense forecast to reflect changes you see happening. Have any costs gone up or down significantly? If you think these changes might be permanent, you can alter your expense forecast to bring it more in line with reality.

    D. If you decide to change any numbers in your forecast, make sure you add everything up again to verify that your business will make a profit in the coming month. If you aren't forecasting a profit for the coming month, do you have a business savings account to cover the shortfall? Do you need to take action now (more marketing, greater emphasis on sales, or cutting costs) to ensure you can make a profit?

Once the firm figures out why the associates were less billable and the partners far more billable than the forecast, the partners may decide to hire a contract person to help with tax preparation. They will re-do the forecast for the next 5 months to include the cost of hiring the additional person, and increase the number of hours they think they will bill using the additional person. They'll rejoice at their good fortune of having so much business, and book their spa appointments for April 16.

12. Finally, set aside time on your calendar to work on your new goals and plans for the coming month. Don't forget to schedule 30 minutes at the end of the next month to do your month-end review, or 90 minutes at the end of next month if it's time to review the whole quarter.

DONE!

The partners have scheduled a catered lunch for a month from today where they will sit down together in their conference room and review the next month's results.

THE QUARTERLY REVIEW PROCESS

In this process we will review both the previous month and the previous three months (the quarter).

Information to gather for the quarterly review:

1. Run the Budget vs. Actual report in your bookkeeping software for the month AND the quarter just ended. If you don't use bookkeeping software, you can do the same thing by hand. Add up all your sales, preferably by product and/or service, so you can see how much of each thing is selling. Then add up all your expenses in each category. Then get out your income and expense forecast and compare what you forecasted would happen against what actually did happen. Do this for both the month and the quarter just past.

2. Make a list of your key measurements for the last month and the last quarter (from Module Eleven).

3. Pull out your whole business plan. You will be reviewing each module to see if the work you did in each module is still true, or if you need to make changes.

Analysis of the Information

Note: the financial analysis for the quarter is the same as the one you do for the month. The difference is that you will be reviewing both the previous month and the previous quarter.

The reason to review the previous quarter is that it is easier to see trends when you are looking at three months at a time. If you have noticed significant changes in your expenses or income, a quarterly review will help you decide if the changes are an aberration or something you need to respond to now.

The other reason to review the whole quarter is that it gives you the opportunity to look at your whole business plan, to make sure it is still guiding your actions and continuing to create clarity as you originally intended.

The financial analysis for the quarter is the same as the one you do for the month. The difference is that you will be reviewing both the previous month and the previous quarter.

Write the answers to the questions that follow in the space below each question. You will use your answers to make changes in your business plan at the end of the review process.

1. Look at your sales, product by product, and/or service by service. Did you sell as much of each as you thought? If the answer is yes, Hurrah for you! Move to the next product/service until you've looked at the sales figures for each one and compared them to what you forecasted when you did your plan. Do this for both the previous month and the previous quarter.

2. If the sales of any product or service are less than your forecast, ask yourself these questions for each product/service that came in lower than you expected, and write your notes in the space below:

    Is this a seasonal blip that happens every year?

    Is this a trend that began last month or the month before?

    If the trend has been building the entire previous quarter, is it time to take action?

3. If you think you need to take action, review the marketing you're doing for this product/service.

    Did you actually do the marketing for this specific product or service this month? Did you do all the marketing during the entire quarter?

If you did do the marketing, did you do enough of it?

If you did enough marketing, do you need to change the marketing you're doing?

4. If your sales are much higher than you forecast for any product or service, ask yourself these questions:

    Does this uptick in sales look like a trend over the previous quarter?

    Should you shift your efforts and marketing dollars over to the product(s)/service(s) that are the most successful and stop spending as much time and effort on the ones not meeting their forecasted numbers?

    Do you have enough infrastructure (employees, your own time, outside contractors, raw materials, etc.) to meet the increased demand?

    Does the data from the quarter give you reason to think that it's time to take action?

5. Next, look at your real expenses for the month and compare them to your forecast. Is anything noticeably out of whack (more than 10% different than what you expected)? Do this for both the previous month and the previous quarter. If you think the information from the previous month or quarter is significant enough to make changes, note the categories that deviated from your forecast in the space below, and any actions you will take to address the issue(s).

6. Now look at your key measurements (from Module Eleven) for both the month and the quarter. Are they on track? I'm assuming that the key measurements you're looking at will be the same for the quarter and the month, but they don't necessarily need to be. In any case, this is the time to ask yourself: do your key measurements still work? Are they giving you insight into what's coming in the next one to two months?

If one of your key measurements shows that sales are down, review your answers to questions 2 and 3 on the previous page and decide if it's time to make some changes, or wait to see what happens in the next month.

If your key measurements are showing increased sales, review your answer to question 4 on the previous page and decide if you need to make changes.

7. Now look at your whole business plan, module by module. Make notes under each question if, after reviewing the module, you need to make changes in your plan.

   A. Module One: Purpose. Is your Purpose still true for you? Do you need to make any changes in it?

   B. Module Two: Vision. Is your Vision the same as it was three months ago? Are you making progress in achieving it? Do you need to make changes?

   C. Module Three: Mission. Is your Mission the same as it was three months ago? Are you still serving the same perfect clients, doing the same work? Do you need to make any changes?

   D. Module Four: Values. Are your Values the same as they were three months ago? Most importantly, are you about to get into any situations, or are you already in any situations that are violating your values? Sometimes it's difficult to see the truth of a situation until you are already mired in it.

   You can tell you are living by your values if you are impressing yourself. If you see that you have become entangled in something that goes against your values, stop now and get some help. If you are in this situation, write down the actions you will take to extricate yourself below:

E. Module Five: Target Market. Are you still serving the same clients? Are your methods of reaching them still working? Are you talking to your new *and* existing clients regularly, in a way that makes sense to them?

F. Module Six: Strategies. Are your strategies still working? Are you using them as a lens to evaluate everything you do in your business? Are you doing anything that is outside your strategies? If so, do you need to alter your strategies to reflect the new reality, or stop doing the thing(s) that don't follow your strategies? (Example: Your strategy is high quality-fair price, but you decided at the spur of the moment to carry parts that are inexpensive and lower quality. Do you want to change your strategy to fit this decision, or get rid of the inexpensive merchandise and stay true to your original strategy?)

G. Module Seven: Unique Selling Proposition. Is it still true? Are you communicating it to your existing and future customers? Are you walking your talk in this area? Are there any changes you need to make to insure that you are still the best?

H. Module Eight: SWOT Analysis. This is a great time to survey your competition again. Are any of them doing things that you think you should be doing? Are there any holes in the market that no one is addressing? Do you have more or less competition than you did last quarter? Have you begun to address the weaknesses you identified last quarter? Have more or different strengths, weaknesses, opportunities, or threats appeared since last quarter? What will you do about them?

I. Modules Nine–Ten–Eleven: the Numbers. Do you need to change your forecast based on your analysis of your numbers? Are your key measurements still helping you see what's going on in your business?

J. Module Twelve: Goals and Plans. Are you on track with your goals for this quarter? Do you need to add/subtract or change any goals and plans for the coming quarter based on the answers to any of the questions above? If you make changes in your goals, note them below. Also make sure that the work you will do to advance your goals gets into your calendar for the coming quarter, whether you change your goals or not.

8. Take your notes from question 7 and incorporate them into your business plan. You can simply edit your original plan to reflect the new information. If you like, you can save the new plan and forecast under a different name (such as Business Plan 1st Quarter 20__) so you can track the changes your plan has undergone over the year.

9. Now take a few minutes and reflect on the changes you've made. If you have any feelings about the changes and you need to talk to someone about what's going on, jot some notes in the space below and make an appointment with the person you will talk to about how you feel or what you think about the changes. The number-one barrier to reviewing the business plan quarterly is the feelings that come up when the plan doesn't match reality. You can talk to your CPA, coach, business partner, action buddy, or whomever else you feel will listen and hold your confidence.

QUARTERLY REVIEW EXAMPLE

This time we will review a clothing manufacturer where things aren't going so well. The business sells to trendy retail boutiques; clothing sales in this segment are down across the country.

1. Run the Budget vs. Actual report in your bookkeeping software for the month AND the quarter just ended. Their income statement for the first quarter is on page 264. The prior month's statement follows on page 265.

2. Make a list of your key measurements:

   Their key measurements are as follows:

   - **Sales price of clothing item compared to forecast.**

   - **Cost of manufacturing clothing item compared to forecast.**

   - **Amount of freight charges as compared to forecast.**

   - **Percentage of returns (target return rate is under 5%).**

   - **General/Administrative expenses actual compared to forecast.**

   - **Net profit as a percentage of total sales (target is: net profit equals at least 10% of sales).**

Analysis of the Information

1. Look at your sales, product by product and/or service by service. Did you sell as much of each as you thought? If the answer is yes, Hurrah for you! Move to the next product/service until you've looked at the sales figures for each one and compared them to what you forecasted when you did your plan. Do this for both the previous month and the previous quarter.

   Things aren't good here. The company sold over a third fewer shirts than they forecasted. Jeans sales are down too, although not by as much.

2. If the sales of any product or service are less than your forecast, ask yourself these questions for each product/service that came in lower than you expected and write your notes in the space below:

Is this a seasonal blip that happens every year?

Is this a trend that began last month or the month before?

If the trend has been building the entire previous quarter, is it time to take action?

This company has been doing its marketing the way that has worked for the last two years, so it isn't that the marketing isn't getting done. Something else is going on.

These lower sales results would make the owner go back and ask more questions of the numbers:

- **Has the downturn in sales been going on in every other month during the last quarter?**

- **Are there some regions or stores that she sells into that are down further than others? (This would require her to break the sales numbers down further, by store or by region).**

She would also ask other questions:

- **Are competitors' sales falling also?**

- **Are her styles no longer fresh? (Perhaps call some stores and ask them for feedback.) Does the marketing need to be changed? (Also ask the stores about this)**

- **Are apparel sales down across every market segment, or are some segments doing better than others?**

- **Should she consider changing her styles for people in her niche, or the more drastic action of changing the niche (her People) altogether?**

3. If you think you need to take action, review the marketing you're doing for this product/service.

Did you actually do the marketing for this specific product or service this month? Did you do all the marketing during the entire quarter?

If you did do the marketing, did you do enough of it?

If you did enough marketing, do you need to change the marketing you're doing?

Her marketing was the same as it has been for the last 2 years; advertising placed in upscale fashion and lifestyle magazines. It is time to talk to her people, her store owners, and ask them what marketing would work better.

4. If your sales are much higher than you forecast in any product or service, ask yourself these questions:

Does this uptick in sales look like a trend over the previous quarter? Should you shift your efforts and marketing dollars over to the product(s)/service(s) that are the most successful and stop spending as much time and effort on the ones not meeting their forecasted numbers?

Do you have enough infrastructure (employees, your own time, outside contractors, raw materials, etc.) to meet the increased demand?

Does the data from the quarter give you reason to think that it's time to take action?

Unfortunately, this is not the problem she is facing.

5.   Next, look at your real expenses for the month and compare them to your forecast. Is anything noticeably out of whack (more than 10% different than what you expected)? Do this for both the previous month and the previous quarter. If you think the information from the previous month or quarter is significant enough to make changes, note the categories that deviated from your forecast in the space below, and any actions you will take to address the issue(s).

Since bad news always likes company, the other measurement that is seriously out of whack is shirt returns. They are three times higher than forecasted in March, and over 20 times higher for the whole quarter. This is a catastrophic problem.

The owner must investigate this problem (and probably already is, since the return rate is lower in March than it has been for the quarter). Is there a quality control issue? A sales problem? Late shipments? Something else, or a combination of all these things?

INCOME STATEMENT FOR THE FIRST QUARTER

	1st quarter forecast	1st quarter actual	Difference
Shirt sale price	150	135	−15
Number sold	5,000	3,200	−1,800
Jeans sales price	$125	$125	$0
Number sold	8,500	8,000	−500

Income	1st quarter forecast	1st quarter actual	Difference
Shirt category	750,000	432,000	−318,000
Cost of goods	225,000	144,000	−81,000
Freight	5,000	3,200	−1,800
Returns	2,250	45,000	−42,750
Gross profit	517,750	239,800	−277,950
Jeans category	1,062,500	1,000,000	−62,500
Cost of goods	340,000	320,000	−20,000
Freight	8,500	8,000	−500
Returns	3,400	6,400	−3,000
Gross profit	710,600	665,600	−45,000
Total gross profit (both categories)	1,228,350	905,400	−322,950
General/admin expenses	892,000	893,000	−1,000
Net profit before taxes	336,350	12,400	−323,950

PRIOR MONTH'S INCOME STATEMENT

	March forecast	*March actual*	*Difference*
Shirt sale price	150	135	−15
Number sold	1,667	1,300	−367
Jeans sales price	$125	$125	$0
Number sold	2,833	2,600	−233

Income	*March forecast*	*March actual*	*Difference*
Shirt category	250,050	175,500	−74,550
Cost of goods	75,000	58,500	−16,500
Freight	1,667	1,300	−367
Returns	750	22,500	−21,750
Gross profit	172,633	93,200	−79,433
Jeans category	354,125	325,000	−29,125
Cost of goods	113,333	104,000	−9,333
Freight	2,833	2,600	−233
Returns	1,133	2,080	−947
Gross profit	236,826	216,320	−20,506
Total gross profit (both categories)	**409,459**	**309,520**	**−99,939**
General/admin expenses	297,333	297,667	−333
Net profit before taxes	**112,126**	**11,853**	**−100,273**

6. Now look at your key measurements (from Module Eleven) for both the month and the quarter. Are they on track?

All her key measurements are income- and expense-related We have talked about each of the problems with sales already, in previous questions.

This brings up the question of adding another key measurement: customer satisfaction. Our owner needs to consider adding this measurement, plus a way to measure the satisfaction, this month.

Tracking customer satisfaction and paying attention to the measurement might have helped her avert the sales slump and horrible return-rate problems; or at least helped her realize there was something wrong before it got this bad.

This is a classic problem for people whose businesses sell to an end consumer, but their product is placed in a store (virtual, or bricks and mortar), by someone else. Our clothing manufacturer needs to be in close touch with, and keep happy, two sets of people, not just one. She needs to have a key measure ment to monitor the happiness of each group.

7. Now look at your whole business plan, module by module. Make notes under each question if, after reviewing the module, you need to make changes in your plan.

   A. Module One: Purpose. Is your Purpose still true for you? Do you need to make any changes in it?

   Her purpose has always been to make beautiful, stylish clothes for young professionals (ages 25–40) who wanted to look like they were wearing designer labels, but didn't want to pay designer prices.

   She is still deeply committed to this purpose. She needs to call her clients (the store owners) and see if her designs are still speaking to the people she wants to clothe.

   B. Module Two: Vision. Is your Vision the same as it was three months ago? Are you making progress in achieving it? Do you need to make changes?

Our owner has a financial vision for the company. Reality (this quarter at least), has not cooperated. She will talk to her clients about what changes in design, manufacturing, and marketing she needs to make to get her sales back on track.

C. Module Three: Mission. Is your Mission the same as it was three months ago? Are you still serving the same people, doing the same work? Do you need to make any changes?

The 25–40-year-old professional woman is the person she is passionate to serve. She is not ready to change this.

D. Module Four: Values. Are your Values the same as they were three months ago? Most importantly, are you about to get into any situations, or are you already in any situations that are violating your values?

Interestingly, she may have caused some of the problems she is experiencing, by violating the value she has lived by since she started the business; to use manufacturing plants that pay decently.

The economy had shown signs of softening last year, so she switched her manufacturing to a different, lower cost plant, even though she didn't approve of the wages they paid. As she investigates the cause(s) of her high returns cost, she may find that cutting corners on manufacturing, something she vowed she wouldn't do, has actually cost her more money.

E. Module Five: Target Market. Are you still serving the same clients? Are your methods of reaching them still working? Are you talking to your new *and* existing clients regularly, in a way that makes sense to them?

This is where the customer satisfaction survey will come in. She has focused her marketing on the end-user; it's now time to pay very close attention to her boutique owners as well.

F. Module Six: Strategies. Are your strategies still working? Are you using them as a lens to evaluate everything you do in your business? Are you doing anything that is outside your strategies?

If so, do you need to alter your strategies to reflect the new reality, or stop doing the thing(s) that don't follow your strategies? (Example: your strategy is high quality-fair price, but you decided at the spur of the moment to carry parts that are inexpensive and lower quality. Do you want to change your strategy to fit this decision, or get rid of the inexpensive merchandise and stay true to your original strategy?)

Our owner's original strategy was to market to end-users only—to draw them into her customers' stores. It looks like this strategy may need to change.

It looks like there might have been a dip in the quality of the clothing as well. This is a values issue (go to manufacturers who pay a living wage), but has also slipped into her strategy, which was to deliver a well-made product.

She doesn't want to change the quality of her clothing, so she will move her manufacturing to a plant that pays workers well. She may change her marketing strategy of only marketing to end-users; she will go talk to her boutique owners and ask them what they want.

G. Module Seven: Unique Selling Proposition. Is it still accurate? Are you communicating it to your existing and future customers? Are you walking your talk in this area? Are there any changes you need to make to insure that you are still the best at your USP?

Illustrating again that a problem with your values can affect other parts of your business (i.e., the manufacturing quality problem), part of her Unique Selling Proposition (great style and construction for a good price) is also threatened. We already know she has to fix this problem; this is simply more confirmation of that fact.

H. Module Eight: SWOT Analysis. This is a great time to survey your competition again. Are any of them doing things that you think you should be doing? Are there any holes in the market that no one is addressing? Do you have more or less competition than you did last quarter? Have you begun to address the weaknesses you identified last quarter? Have more or different strengths, weaknesses, opportunities, or threats appeared since last quarter? What will you do about them?

Besides the quality problem that I have beaten to death (which she would file under "weaknesses," and fix), this module is the place to go out and survey both the competition, and the economy. What's going on in her market segment? How are competitors responding? Once she has gathered this information, she can go back and make sure her marketing is working, her prices are in line, her client relationships are strong, and her designs are still popular.

I. Modules Nine–Ten–Eleven: the Numbers. Do you need to change your forecast based on your analysis of your numbers? Are your key measurements still helping you see what's going on in your business?

The key measurements are working with the exception of adding one to measure customer satisfaction.

The big question here is whether to revise the forecast or not. I think the answer is yes. It will take her a couple of months to straighten out the quality problem; in the meantime, she needs to lower the forecast to reflect what's really happening right now. She may also need to look at her expenses, to see what can be put off, cut out, or reduced.

If she can't cut expenses fast enough, can't, or won't, lay off key employees because she feels the downturn will be short-lived, she might decide to draw on her business savings account, to get her through the next couple of months. This decision must not be made in a vacuum; she will talk the situation over with her support people (CPA, coach, mastermind group), or whomever she trusts.

J. Module Twelve: Goals and Plans. Are you on track with your goals for this quarter? Do you need to add/subtract or change any goals and plans for the coming quarter based on the answers to any of the questions above? If you make changes in your goals, note them below. Also make sure that the work you will do to advance your goals gets into your calendar for the coming quarter, whether you change your goals or not.

Her Goals and Plans this quarter were to start shopping for new computer software and a larger office.

Instead, she will spend at least the next month, and possibly the next quarter, understanding her manufacturing issues, changing manufacturing plants, and visiting her store owners, either in person or on the phone. Depending on how that goes in the month to come, she may continue this work the whole quarter. Her revised Goals and Plans look like this:

Goal: Fix manufacturing problem

Plan: Talk to the ten stores who have the highest returns and find out what the problem is, by April 15

Plan: Interview 3 new potential manufacturing plants by April 30

Plan: Examine contract in place with existing manufacturer to see if there is any recourse to them by April 5

Plan: Decide on new plant by May 5

Plan: Move manufacturing to new plant by June 1

Goal: Institute new customer-satisfaction process for store owners

Plan: Talk to top ten store owners by April 10, get feedback on problems, ask them how they want the company to keep in touch with them, how problem resolution is going, gather all information necessary to create new process.

Plan: List all problems store owners reported, meet with staff to fix them by April 30

Plan: Send "fix" report by May 10

Plan: Create new customer-satisfaction survey based on store owner feedback by May 30, implement June 1.

This means the other goals and plans for the coming quarter will have to be pushed off to later in the year.

8. Take your notes from question 7 and incorporate them into your business plan. You can simply edit your original plan to reflect the new information. If you like, you can save the new plan and forecast under a different name (such as Business Plan 1st Quarter 2009) so you can track the changes your plan has undergone over the year.

   She will revise her forecast down for the next quarter, incorporate the new customer-satisfaction system and key measurement into the plan, redistribute the previous plans she made for the quarter into later in the year, and communicate the new business plan to her key employees and advisors.

9. Now take a few minutes and reflect on the changes you've made. If you have any feelings about the changes and you need to talk to someone about what's going on, jot some notes in the space below and make an appointment with the person you will talk to about how you feel or what you think about the changes. The number-one barrier to reviewing the business plan quarterly is the feelings that come up when the plan doesn't match reality. You can talk to your CPA, coach, business partner, action buddy, or whomever else you feel will listen and hold your confidence.

   It can be very painful to hit a business downturn, no matter what the reason. It's important to remember your purpose, keep in touch with your clients and do what they want, and stick to your values (as well as sticking to the rest of your plan).

   It's easy to get seduced by negativity; make sure if (or when) you get into this situation, that you stay connected with what's really happening (a CPA is really good at helping with this), and change the things you have power over.

   Not every business stays in business. By doing your monthly and quarterly reviews (as well as creating your business plan and revising it as you get new information), your chances of survival and prosperity are much increased.

The Final Note

It takes courage, perseverance and even some luck to make it to the end of a book like this. Courage to do what Henry David Thoreau talked about; putting foundations under your dreams, and perseverance to keep going in the face of uncertainty about whether your dreams will turn out the way you hope. Plus luck; especially if you found people to work through the book with, who gave you honest feedback and stuck with it until everyone finished their business plans. Bravo. Most people never get even halfway to making their dreams real.

I often read the end of a book first to decide if I want to read from the beginning and do the work. It's okay if you did that too.

Whichever way you landed on this page, I'd like you to know that one of the scariest and most difficult tasks on earth is the one you're doing right now: making your ideas real. Our ideas never look the way we think they're going to when we first conceive them. Reality always has the final say. You've signed up to take someone to the dance who will always lead. You'll need to learn how to be a skilled, supple, adaptable follower.

Once you know this, however, it makes the process of manifesting your ideas a bit easier. Once you know they'll never turn out the way you think they will, once you realize that your business plan is simply a rough (but crucial) map over uncharted terrain, I hope you (and I) can let go. Let go of the grip we have on things turning out the way we think they should, and be grateful for the way they actually do turn out. Our job is to draw the map, begin to follow it, then revise it as we see what the terrain really looks like.

But you can't start the process without a map, no matter how incomplete it turns out to be. Making the map is our job. Congratulations if you finished yours; if you didn't, go find someone and finish your maps together. I gave directions in the book for people who try to do it alone, but truthfully, that's almost impossible. Give yourself the gift of doing the work with someone.

The working title for this book was Making It Real. There's something sacred about taking an idea that you love and trying to do that; to make something real that's not existed before.

I hope you find this book helpful in your process of creating something the world has not yet seen. Your work matters.

Index

About the Author

Christy Strauch earned an MBA from UCLA, went to work at a Fortune 500 company, then ran her own (non-Fortune 500) IT company for 16 years. During that time she experienced first-hand how a bad relationship with money and business polluted everything else: her bonds with other people, her peace of mind, and her creativity. From that experience her coaching practice was born 15 years ago. Her mission is helping creatives make a peaceful relationship with business and money so they can get their work into the world.

Her next book, *Artists: Don't Starve!,* addresses the number one reason why creatives struggle with money: trauma, and shows what to do about that. She lives in Scottsdale, AZ and when not writing, teaching, speaking and coaching, she hikes, travels and plays the ukulele (just not all at the same time).

Made in the USA
Las Vegas, NV
05 February 2023

66918392R00171